The Daily Office

A Book of Hours for Daily Prayer

After the Use of THE ORDER OF SAINT LUKE

for

Lent and the Triduum

Dwight W. Vogel, O.S.L.
Editor and Compiler

Issued: Lent, 1993

ORDER OF SAINT LUKE PUBLICATIONS
Cleveland, Ohio

THE DAILY OFFICE
A Book of Hours for Daily Prayer
After the Use of THE ORDER OF SAINT LUKE
for Lent and the Triduum

Copyright © 1993 by the Order of Saint Luke
All rights reserved

ISBN 1-878009-13-3

This book is printed on acid-free paper that meets the American
National Standards Institute Z39.48 Standard

Produced and manufactured in the United States of America by

Order of Saint Luke Publications
P.O. Box 27425 - Cleveland, Ohio 44127-0425

Production Editing: Timothy J.Crouch, O.S.L.

The Order of Saint Luke invites people throughout the church to use these offices. We also solicit comments based upon their use. Please direct all comments and suggestions to the Publishing Office.

THE DAILY OFFICE

TABLE OF CONTENTS

PREFACE

The Order of Saint Luke is a religious order in the United Methodist Church dedicated to sacramental and liturgical scholarship, education and practice. In 1988, the Order published *The Book of Offices and Services* to provide resources for its members in their commitment to daily prayer. That same year the General Chapter established a task force to develop additional resources for daily prayer.

There are many who pray daily in a variety of ways. Our intent is to reclaim the practice of praying the "daily office" — a pattern of praise, prayer, scripture and reflection related to the historic "hours" — specified times for focusing our prayer.

The first volume provided for praying the daily office from the beginning of Advent through the Baptism of Our Lord. It was received with great appreciation, for which we are thankful to God. We have tried to respond to your suggestions in this volume, which will help us pray together through "holy lent" and those high holy days of the Christian year which the ancient church called the "triduum."

Our work has been guided by the following presuppositions:

1. The Order of St. Luke, while a religious community, lives most of its life in dispersion. Thus, even in areas of the country where there are active chapters, daily prayer will more often be a "solitary" office than a "corporate one." The offices of daily prayer must, therefore, be meaningful when used by individual members.

2. The daily prayer of the order is an essential expression of community, even when in dispersion. The order for daily prayer must, therefore, engender a sense of community prayer even when prayed alone. It must also be able to provide a significant resource for use when members of the order are able to meet together.

We have tried to omit words which would not make sense when spoken to one's self (e.g. "The Lord be with you; and also with you"). However, we have not tried to eliminate the use of the plural (inherent in "Our Father" but not restricted to that reminder of *koinonia*). We have continued to include the use of bold-faced type for those occasions when the prayers are prayed together, believing that they do not "get in the way" when praying a solitary office.

When prayed in community, collects and times of prayer should be introduced with the following dialogue:

The Lord be with you.
And also with you.
Let us pray.

3. Repetition provides for a depth of appropriation not available when constant change is the basic pattern; yet the continual repetition of fixed content can lead to boredom and emptiness. Thus, what is "ordinary" and what is "proper" must be kept in a creative balance. The "ordinary" seeks to reflect those parts of the daily office which have stood the test of time. Thus, the use of the traditional canticles and the evening hymn in the ordinary of the offices is maintained.

4. We have sought to be inclusive in our references to human beings, and to reflect the rich heritage available to us in the naming of our God who is beyond all names. We have followed the pattern established by the Order of St. Luke in adopting *The Book of Offices and Services* by using the doxological form of the Eastern church: "Glory to the blessed and holy Trinity."

The **ordinary** includes offices or services for seven of the traditional "hours" for prayer. The complete cycle can be used when on retreat, at times when spiritual discipline is important to our growth, or as a reminder that day and night can be permeated with prayer. An office which may be used at any time as a guide for daily prayer is provided (see Rite Two), and the historic Great Litany based on the litany of Thomas Cranmer is included as well.

Individuals and chapters are encouraged to use these offices as guides and resources, and to develop appropriate adaptations in light of needs and circumstances. You are encouraged to share with us your reflections regarding the work we have done.

We have chosen not to provide a lectionary for all the offices. Some of our members are helped by using the lections for the following Sunday during the preceding week. Others prefer to use the lectionary from *The Book of Common Prayer*, the *Lutheran Book of Worship*, or W. Douglas Mills' *A Daily Lectionary*. We encourage those using this resource to follow the lections listed in sources such as these. For certain offices, especially those of the triduum we have provided suggested lections.

The editor wishes to express special appreciation to Brother Thomas A. Rand, O.S.L. who served as editorial assistant, and to Garrett-Evangelical Theological Seminary for their support of this project.

We share our work with you in the name of the blessed and holy Trinity. "Unless the Lord builds the house, they labor in vain who build it."

Dwight W. Vogel, O.S.L.
Garrett-Evangelical Theological Seminary
2121 Sheridan Road
Evanston, IL 60201

Contributors:
Daniel T. Benedict, O.S.L.
Barbara Braley, O.S.L.
Timothy J. Crouch, O.S.L.
Elmer Lee Eveland, O.S.L.
Allan J. Ferguson, O.S.L.
Sarah Flynn, O.S.L.
Gregory L. Hayes, O.S.L.
Schuyler J. Lowe-McCracken, O.S.L.
William P. McDonald, O.S.L.
Brian O'Grady, O.S.L.
Thomas A. Rand, O.S.L.
Dwight W. Vogel, O.S.L.

Advisory Member: Abbot Michael J. O'Donnell, O.S.L.

Ordinary Of The Hours

Together with Seasonal Propers

EVENING PRAYER
(Vespers or Evensong)

ENTRANCE OF THE LIGHT   *(See propers for the day)*
Light and peace in Jesus Christ!
Thanks be to God!

HYMN OF LIGHT   *(Phos hilaron)*

Reprinted from *Lutheran Book of Worship*. Copyright © 1978. by permission of Augsburg Fortress

O gracious Light,
  pure brightness of our everlasting God in heaven,
O Jesus Christ,
  holy and blessed!
Now as we come to the setting of the sun,
  and our eyes behold the vesper light,
we sing your praises, O God:
  most holy and blessed Trinity.
You are worthy at all times
  to be praised with happy voices,
O Son of God, O Giver of Life,
  and to be glorified through all the worlds.
[ADAPTED BY TJC FROM THE WORK OF CHARLES MORTIMER GUILBERT]

[THANKSGIVING FOR LIGHT (On Saturday and Sunday evenings)

[INCENSE
[An angel, holding a golden censer full of incense, stood
[before the altar. The smoke of the incense went up before
[God, mingled with the prayers of the people. (REVELATION 8:3-4)\

8

EVENING PRAYER CANTICLE (selected from Psalm 141)

A. Chant Form:

Reprinted from *Lutheran Book of Worship*. Copyright © 1978. by permission of Augsburg Fortress

Antiphon: **My prayers <u>rise</u> like incense;**
my hands like the <u>eve</u>ning sacrifice.

(See *UMH*, bottom of p. 850 for musical setting by Arlo Duba)

I call to you, O God, come <u>to</u> me quickly;
  Hear my voice when I <u>cry</u> to you.
Let my prayer rise before <u>you</u> like incense,
  and my hands like the <u>eve</u>ning sacrifice.
Keep guard over my <u>mouth</u>, O Lord;
  watch the door <u>of</u> my lips.
Keep my heart from slipping <u>in</u>to evil;
  let me not be busy with <u>evil</u>doers.
My eyes are turned toward you, O <u>Lord</u> my God.
  In you I take refuge; do not deprive <u>me</u> of life.

[Trans. Arlo D. Duba; © Arlo D. Duba, 1986; Printed by permission.]

Antiphon

B: Metrical Form: [88.88.88; tune: SELENA, *UMH* 287]

Come quickly, Lord, I call on you;
And hear my voice, my cry for help.
Control my lips and tongue, O Lord,
And save my heart from evil's grasp.
  Let my prayer rise like incense, Lord,
  My hands, an ev'ning sacrifice.

Help me accept rebuke as grace,
And guard me from all bitterness.
All wicked ways may I resist
And never share in sensuous feasts.
    Let my prayer rise like incense, Lord,
    My hands, an ev'ning sacrifice.

Protect me from the Evil One,
And rule my life through Christ your Son,
With Holy Fire my sins consume,
And flood my soul with love divine,
    My heart shall rise as incense, Lord,
    My life, your living sacrifice.   [SF]

CONFESSION AND PARDON (See propers for the day)

PSALTER
    O God, make speed to save us.
    O Lord, hasten to help us.
    Glory to you, O Trinity, most holy and blessed;
    One God, now and forever. Amen.
        (See propers for the day)

SCRIPTURE(S) and SILENT REFLECTION

CANTICLE OF MARY   (*Magnificat*; Luke 1:39-56)
    (See *UMH* 197 st. 4 or 198-200 for metrical versions)

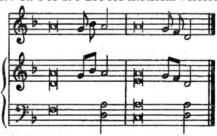

Reprinted from *Lutheran Book of Worship.* Copyright © 1978. by permission of Augsburg Fortress

My soul proclaims your greatness, Lord;
    my spirit rejoices in you, my Savior;
For you have looked with favor on your lowly servant;
**   from this day all generations will call me blessed.**

10

You, the Almighty, have done great <u>things</u> for me;
and holy <u>is</u> your name.
You have mercy on <u>those</u> who fear you
in every <u>gen</u>eration.
You have shown the strength <u>of</u> your arm;
You have scattered the proud in <u>their</u> conceit.
You have cast the mighty <u>from</u> their thrones;
You have lifted <u>up</u> the lowly.

You have filled the hungry <u>with</u> good things;
and the rich have been sent <u>a</u>way empty.
You have come to the help of your <u>ser</u>vant Israel;
for you have remembered your <u>promise</u> of mercy,
the promise you made <u>to</u> our forebears;
to Abraham and his <u>children</u> for ever.   [ADAPTED, TJC]

[READING(S) FOR MEDITATION AND REFLECTION

P R A Y E R S   (See propers for the day)

SILENT PRAYER

[OTHER SELECTED PRAYERS
         (From the following or other resource)
THE COLLECT FOR PEACE
    Most holy God, the source of all good desires, all
    right judgements, and all just works; Give to us,
    your servants, that peace which the world cannot
    give, so that our minds may be fixed on the doing of
    your will, and the fear of our enemies having been
    removed, we may pass our time in rest and quiet-
    ness; Through the mercies of Jesus Christ our Savior.
    Amen.   [GELASIAN SACRAMENTARY, ALT, TJC]

THE COLLECT FOR AID AGAINST PERILS

O God, the life of all who live, the light of the faithful, the strength of those who labor, and the repose of the dead: We thank you for the blessings of the day that is past and humbly ask for your protection through the coming night. Bring us in safety to the morning hours; Through him who died and rose again for us, our Savior Jesus Christ. **Amen.**

[**PRAYERS OF SPECIAL INTENTION** (such as the following:)

A COLLECT FOR THE ORDER OF ST. LUKE

O Shepherd of us all, whose gifts are that some should be pastors and teachers: grant, we ask you, your Spirit to the Order of Saint Luke, that we may faithfully administer your holy Word and Sacraments and bring your healing grace to those committed to our care; through Jesus Christ our Lord. **Amen.**

or

O Shepherd of us all, who inspired your servant Saint Luke the physician to set forth in the Gospel the love and healing power of Jesus: Grant, we ask you, your Spirit to the Order of Saint Luke, that we may proclaim faithfully the Apostolic hope, magnify the Sacraments, and bring your healing grace to the whole Church; Through the same Jesus Christ our Lord. **Amen.**

CONCLUDING COLLECT (See propers for the day)

THE LORD'S PRAYER   (See *UMH* 270-271 for musical settings)

[HYMN (See propers for the day)

GOING FORTH (See propers for the day)

COMPLINE

(Night Prayer)

CALL TO PRAYER

O God, come to our assistance.
O Lord, hasten to help us.
The Lord almighty grant us a restful night,
and peace at the last.
Amen.

NIGHT HYMN

[LM, Tune: *CONDITOR ALME* (*UMH* 692)
or *MARYTON* (*UMH* 430)]

O Christ, who art the Light and Day,
Thou drivest night and gloom away;
O Light of Light, whose word doth show
The light of heav'n to us below.

All-holy Lord, in humble prayer
We ask tonight thy watchful care;
O grant us calm repose in thee,
A quiet night from perils free.

Asleep though wearied eyes may be,
Still keep the heart awake to thee;
Let thy right hand outstretched above
Guard those who serve the Lord they love.

All praise to God our Abba be,
All praise, eternal Christ, to thee,
Whom with the Spirit we adore,
For ever and for evermore.

[AN AMBROSIAN HYMN MENTIONED IN THE RULE OF ST. CAESARIUS, C. AD 502;
TR. *HYMNS ANCIENT AND MODERN* COMPILERS, 1904]

PRAYER OF CONFESSION

O God, to you we confess our sins and shortcomings.
We are so ready to judge the world
while unable to examine ourselves.

13

We soon forget Christ's forty days in the wilderness,
where he prayed and listened for your voice and
direction.
We have turned away from you, and instead turned to
ourselves.
Forgive us, O God.
Speak to our hearts, so that we might speak to the world,
serving your people faithfully.

--silent reflection and confession--

In the name of Jesus Christ, we are forgiven.
Thanks be to God. Amen.   [SJM]

PSALTER
Our help is in the name of the Lord;
who made heaven and earth.
Glory to the blessed and holy Trinity,
One God, now and forever. Amen.

(Psalm 91, 4, 134, 139:1-12, 34:1-14, 124, or 121)

SCRIPTURE   (A brief passage such as the following:)
We do not live to ourselves, and we do not die to
ourselves. If we live, we live to the Lord, and if we die,
we die to the Lord; so that, whether we live or whether
we die, we are the Lord's. For to this end Christ died and
lived again, so that he might be Lord of both the dead
and the living.   (ROMANS 14:7-9 NRSV)

The Word of the Lord.
Thanks be to God!

SILENT REFLECTION

PRAYERS
THE *KYRIE* (See *UMH* 482-484 for musical settings)
Lord, have mercy upon us.
Christ, have mercy upon us.
Lord, have mercy upon us.

PRAYER FOR THE NIGHT

Visit this place, O Lord, and deliver us from every
snare of the enemy. May your angels be round about
us to guard us in peace and let your blessing be upon
us always; through Christ our Lord. **Amen.**

[ROMAN BREVIARY, ALT.]

COLLECT   (One of the following:)

Watch, dear Lord, with those who wake, or watch, or
weep tonight, and give your angels charge over
those who sleep. Tend your sick ones, O Lord Christ.
Rest your weary ones. Bless your dying ones. Soothe
your suffering ones. Pity your afflicted ones. Shield
your joyous ones. And all, for your Love's sake.
Amen.   [ST. AUGUSTINE, 4TH C.]

O Lord, be within us, to strengthen us, without us to
keep us. O Lord, be above us, to protect us, beneath us
to uphold us. O Lord, be before us to direct us, behind
us to keep us from straying, round about us to defend
us. Blessed are you, O Lord, most holy, forever and ever.
Amen.   [BISHOP LANCELOT ANDREWS, 1585-1626]

THE LORD'S PRAYER   (See *UMH* 270-271 for musical settings)

HYMN   [84.84.888.4; Tune: *AR HYD Y NOS ,UMH* 688]

God that madest earth and heaven,
  darkness and light,
who the day for toil hast given, for rest the night.
May thine angel guards defend us,
slumber sweet thy mercy send us,
holy dreams and hopes attend us
this live-long night.

When the constant sun returning unseals our eyes,
may we born anew like morning, to labor rise.
Gird us for the task that calls us,
let not ease and self enthrall us,
strong through thee whate'er befall us,
O God most wise!   [REGINALD HEBER, 1783-1826]

COMMENDATION

In peace we will lie down and sleep.
In the Lord alone we safely rest.
Guide us waking, O Lord, and guard us sleeping,
that awake we may watch with Christ,
and asleep we may rest in peace.
May the divine help remain with us always.
And with those who are absent from us.

- silence -

Into your hands, O Lord, I commend my spirit,
For you have redeemed me, O Lord,
O God of Truth.

[ADAPTED FROM PS. 4:8, THE SARUM BREVIARY, AND PS. 30:5, TJC]

CANTICLE OF SIMEON (*Nunc Dimittis*; Luke 2:29-32)
(See *UMH* 225-226 for metrical versions)

Reprinted from *Lutheran Book of Worship*. Copyright © 1978. by permission of Augsburg Fortress

Lord, you have now set your <u>ser</u>vant free
to go in peace as <u>you</u> have promised;
for these eyes of mine have <u>seen</u> the Savior,
Whom you have prepared for all the <u>world</u> to see.
A Light to en<u>light</u>en the nations,
And the glory of your <u>peo</u>ple Israel.   [ICET]

GOING FORTH

May Almighty God, the blessed and holy Trinity,
guard and bless us.
Thanks be to God! Amen.

16

VIGIL
(Mid-Night Matins)

[See propers for the day for Vigils for Ash Wednesday p. 42, Holy Thursday (p. 115), Good Friday (p. 132), and the Great Paschal Vigil (p. 144]

OPENING DIALOGUE

O Lord, open my lips,
  my mouth shall proclaim Your praise.
O God, come to my assistance.
  O Lord, hasten to help me.
Glory to you, O Trinity, most holy and blessed:
  one God, now and forever. Amen.

CANTICLE OF PRAISE TO GOD (*Venite Exultemus*)
(For a four-part musical version, see *UMH* 91)

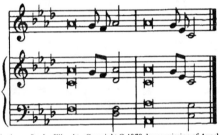

Reprinted from *Lutheran Book of Worship.* Copyright © 1978. by permission of Augsburg Fortress

O come, let us sing <u>to</u> the Lord;
  let us heartily rejoice in the strength of <u>our</u> salvation.
Let us come into God's presence <u>with</u> thanksgiving,
  and show that we are <u>glad</u> with psalms.
For God is a great God, and a great sovereign a<u>bove</u> all gods,
  In whose hands are all the corners of the earth,
  and the strength <u>of</u> the hills.
The sea is <u>God's</u> who made it;
  whose hands prepared <u>the</u> dry land.

O come, let us worshi<u>p</u> <u>and</u> fall down,
  and kneel before the <u>Lord</u> our Maker;

For the Lord <u>is</u> our God;
  we are the people of God's pasture,
  and the sheep <u>of</u> God's hand.
In the beauty of holiness, <u>worship</u> the Lord
  Of whom the whole earth <u>stands</u> in awe.
For the Lord comes, for the Lord comes to <u>judge</u>
  the earth,
  to judge the world with righteousness,
  and <u>peoples</u> with truth.

Glory to you, O Trinity, most <u>holy</u> and blessed;
  One God, now and for <u>ever.</u> Amen.

[Ps. 95:1-7; 96:9, 13; ALT. DWV]

THE BLESSING

Lord, grant us your blessing.
  **May God light the fire of divine love in our hearts.
  Amen.**

THE LESSONS

[In a long vigil, nine lessons may be read. They may be taken from the psalms, be selected according to the season, or be *lectio continua* (continuing readings taken from one Biblical book). On holy festivals, the readings proclaim salvation history (see propers for the day). Each reading is followed by a time of silence.]

[Otherwise, three brief lessons may be read, each followed by a time of silence. The last reading should call forth the praise of the church in the following canticle.]

CANTICLE OF THE HOLY TRINITY (*Te Deum Laudamus*)

Adapted by DWV from Lutheran Book of Worship., copyright ©1978, by permission of Augsburg Fortress

You are <u>God</u>: we praise you!
  You are the Lord: <u>we</u> acclaim you.

18

You are the eternal God who <u>has</u> created:
All creation <u>wor</u>ships you.
To you all angels, all the <u>pow'rs</u> of heaven,
Cherubim and Seraphim, sing in <u>end</u>less praise:
Holy, holy, holy Lord, God of <u>pow'r</u> and might,
heaven and earth are full <u>of</u> your glory.

The glorious company of a<u>pos</u>tles praise you.
The noble fellowship of <u>pro</u>phets praise you.
The white-robed army of <u>mar</u>tyrs praise you.
Throughout the world the holy <u>Church</u> acclaims you;
O cre-a-tor God, of majes<u>ty</u> unbounded,
Your true and only Son, worthy of all worship,
and the Holy Spirit, advo<u>cate</u> and guide.

You Christ, <u>reign</u> in glory,
the eternal <u>Son</u> of God.
When you came in the flesh to <u>set</u> us free
You did not shun the <u>Virgin</u>'s womb.
You overcame the <u>sting</u> of death
And opened heaven to <u>all</u> believers.
You are seated at God's right <u>hand</u> in glory.
We believe that you will come to <u>be</u> our judge.

Come then Lord, and help your people,
bought with the price of <u>your</u> own blood,
And bring us with your saints to glory <u>ev</u>erlasting.

<small>[THE "AMBROSIAN HYMN;" ATTRIBUTED TO BISHOP NICETA (c392-414); ADAPTED BY TJC]</small>

THE LORD'S PRAYER (See *UMH* 270-271 for musical settings)

CONCLUDING PRAYERS
O Lord, hear my prayer,
And let my cry come to you.
Listen to the prayers of your servants;
have mercy on us, Lord Jesus Christ.
Let us bless the Lord.
Thanks be to God!
May the souls of the faithful departed,
through the mercy of God, rest in peace.
Amen.

MORNING PRAYER
(Lauds)

CALL TO PRAISE AND PRAYER
    O Lord, open my lips,
      And my mouth shall proclaim your praise.
    We praise you, O God.
      Your holy name be praised!
        (See propers of the day)

HYMN (See propers of the day)

MORNING PRAYER (See propers of the day)

PSALTER (See propers of the day)
    Glory to the blessed and holy Trinity:
      One God now and forever. Amen.

SCRIPTURE READING(S) AND SILENT REFLECTION

CANTICLE OF ZECHARIAH (*Benedictus*, Luke 1:68-70)
      (See *UMH* 208, 209 for metrical versions)

Adapted by DWV from Lutheran Book of Worship, copyright ©1978, by permission of Augsburg Fortress

Blessed be the Lord, the God of I̲srael,
    Who has come to set the chosen peo̲ple free.
    The Lord has raised u̲p for us
      a mighty Savior from the hou̲se of David.
    Through the holy prophets,
    God promised of old to save us from our e̲nemies,
      from the hands of a̲ll who hate us;
    to show mercy t̲o our forebears
      and to remember the ho̲ly covenant.

This was the oath God swore to our <u>father</u> Abraham;
   to set us free from the hands of our <u>ene</u>mies,
free to worship with<u>out</u> fear,
   holy and righteous in the Lord's sight,
   all the days <u>of</u> our life.
And you, child, shall be called the prophet of <u>the</u> Most
   High,
   for you will go before the Lord to pre<u>pare</u> the way,
to give God's people knowledge <u>of</u> salvation
   by the forgiveness <u>of</u> their sins.
In the tender compassion <u>of</u> our God
   the dawn from on high shall <u>break</u> upon us,
to shine on those who dwell in darkness and the <u>shadow</u> of
death,
      and to guide our feet into the <u>way</u> of peace.   [ICET]

[READING(S) FOR MEDITATION AND REFLECTION

P R A Y E R S   (See propers of the day)

SILENT PRAYER AND/OR FREE PRAYER

[OTHER SELECTED PRAYERS
   (From the following or other resources)

THE COLLECT FOR PEACE
Almighty God,
from whom all thoughts of truth and peace do come:
Pour into the hearts of all people, we pray,
the true love of peace;
and guide with your wisdom
those who take counsel for the nations of the earth,
that in tranquility your work may go forward
until the world is filled with the knowledge of your love;
Through Jesus Christ our Lord. **Amen.**

[BISHOP FRANCIS PAGET, 1851-1911, ALT TJC]

21

THE COLLECT FOR GRACE

O God, by whom we are guided in judgement,
and who raises up for us light in the darkness:
Grant us, in all our doubts and uncertainties,
the grace to ask what you would have us to do;
that your Spirit of Wisdom may save us from all false
choices,
and in your straight path we may not stumble;
Through Jesus Christ our Lord. **Amen.**

[JOHN W. SUTER, JR., INSPIRED BY IS. 30:15 AND PS. 46:11; FROM *SERVICES FOR TRIAL USE: SERIES THREE, 1973,* OF THE CHURCH OF ENGLAND; ALT TJC]

[**PRAYERS OF SPECIAL INTENTION** (such as the following:)

A COLLECT FOR THE ORDER OF ST. LUKE

O Shepherd of us all,
who inspired your servant Saint Luke the physician
to set forth in the Gospel the love and healing power of
Jesus:
Grant, we ask you, your Spirit to the Order of Saint Luke,
that we may proclaim faithfully the Apostolic hope,
magnify the Sacraments,
and bring your healing grace to the whole Church;
Through the same Jesus Christ our Lord. **Amen.**

CONCLUDING COLLECT   (See propers for the day)

THE LORD'S PRAYER (See *UMH* 270-271 for musical settings)

SONG OF PRAISE (See propers for the day)

DISMISSAL AND BLESSING
   OR ASCRIPTION OF PRAISE
   (See propers for the day)

MID-MORNING PRAYER

(Terce)

OPENING DIALOGUE

O God, come to our assistance.
O Lord, hasten to help us.
Glory to the blessed and holy Trinity;
One God now and forever. Amen.

PRAYER

Holy Spirit,
Come upon us this hour without delay;
Pour out your graces on our souls.
Let tongue and soul and mind and strength proclaim
your praise.
Set our love aflame by the fire of your love,
and may its warmth enkindle love in our neighbors.
Empower us with your presence
in the name of Christ. **Amen.**

[FROM THE HYMN FOR THIS HOUR ATTRIBUTED TO ST. AMBROSE, 340-397, ADAPTED BY DWV]

[PSALTER Psalm 90

THE "LITTLE CHAPTER"

Thus says the LORD, who created you O Jacob,
Thus says the Lord who formed, O Israel:
Do not fear, for I have redeemed you;
I have called you by name, you are mine.
When you pass through the waters, I will be with you;
**and through the rivers, they shall not overwhelm
you;**
when you walk through fire you shall not be burned,
and the flame shall not consume you.
For I am the LORD your God,
the Holy One of Israel, your Savior.   (ISAIAH 43: 1-3A)

A Brief Time of Silence

[FREE PRAYER

THE LORD'S PRAYER (See *UMH* 270, 271 for musical settings)

CONCLUDING PRAYER:
Living God, in whom we live and move and have our
being:
Guide and govern us by your Holy Spirit,
so that in all the cares and occupations of our life
we may not forget you,
but remember that we are ever walking in your sight;
through Jesus Christ our Lord. **Amen.**   [BCP, ALT. DWV]

MID-DAY PRAYER

(Sext)

OPENING SENTENCES
> O God, come to our assistance.
> **O Lord, hasten to help us.**
> Glory to the blessed and holy Trinity;
> **One God now and forever. Amen.**

ACT OF PRAISE

Reprinted from *Lutheran Book of Worship*, copyright ©1978, by permission of Augsburg Fortress

> Praise the Lord! Praise, O servants of the Lord,
> Praise the name of the Lord!

> Blessed be the name of the Lord
> from this time forth and for evermore.
> From the rising of the sun to its setting
> the name of the Lord is to be praised!   (PSALM 113:1-4)

COLLECT   (one of the following)
> Living and dying, Lord, we would be yours; keep us
> yours forever, and draw us day by day nearer to your-
> self, until we are wholly filled with your love and fitted
> to behold you, face to face. **Amen.**
>
> [ADAPTED FROM A PRAYER BY EDWARD BOUVERIE PUSEY; DTB]

> Grant, Almighty God, that we, who deserve your judg-
> ment, by the comfort of your grace may mercifully be
> relieved; through our Lord and Savior Jesus Christ.
> **Amen.**   [ADAPTED FROM BCP, 1879; SJM]

25

THE *KYRIE*   (See *UMH* 482-484 for musical settings)
Lord, have mercy upon us.
   Christ, have mercy upon us.
Lord, have mercy upon us.

[SCRIPTURE(S)   (Selected)

THE "LITTLE CHAPTER"
Even those who are young grow weak;
   the young can fall exhausted.
But those who wait on the Lord for help
will find their strength renewed.
   They will rise on wings like eagles;
they will run and not get weary;
   they will walk and not grow weak.   (ISAIAH 40:30-31)

A Brief Time of Silence

[FREE PRAYER

THE LORD'S PRAYER (See *UMH* 270, 271 for musical settings)

CONCLUDING PRAYER:
Send forth your Spirit, Lord,
   Renew the face of the earth.
Creator Spirit, come,
   Inflame our waiting hearts.
Lord, hear our prayer.
   And let our cry come to You.
Bless the Lord.
   Thanks be to God!

MID-AFTERNOON PRAYER

(None)

OPENING SENTENCES
> O God, come to our assistance.
> **O Lord, hasten to help us.**
> Glory to the blessed and holy Trinity;
> **One God now and forever. Amen.**

PRAYER
> Living, loving God:
> Through your wisdom the hours of the day move on,
> and there is yet much to do.
> Keep us in your care and renew us with your strength
> so that we may not forget you
> nor be unaware of your love towards those around us.
> In the name of Christ who lives and reigns
> with you and the Holy Spirit, **Amen.**   [DWV]

[PSALTER Psalm 107:1-9, 33-43

THE "LITTLE CHAPTER"
> Do not remember the former things,
> **or consider the things of old.**
> I am about to do a new thing;
> **now it springs forth, do you not perceive it?**
> I will make a way in the wilderness and rivers in the desert.
> **The wild animals will honor me,**
> **the jackals and the ostriches;**
> For I give water in the wilderness, rivers in the desert.
> to give drink to my chosen people,
> **the people whom I formed for myself**
> **so that they might declare my praise.**   (ISAIAH 43: 18-21)

A Brief Time of Silence

[FREE PRAYER

THE LORD'S PRAYER (See *UMH* 270, 271 for musical settings)

CONCLUDING PRAYER:
Lord Jesus Christ,
who came to set us free:
Let the shadow of your cross fall upon us in this hour
that we may wonder at the gift of your redeeming
love,
and be empowered by your Spirit
to take up our own cross daily
and follow you. **Amen.**   [DWV]

CONCLUDING PRAYER
Show us, O Lord, your mercy,
And grant us your salvation.
Bless the Lord!
Thanks be to God!

RITE TWO

(A general outline which may be used at any time)
Adapted from
The Book of Offices and Services of The Order of St. Luke

CALL TO WORSHIP

(See "Calls to Praise and Prayer" in Morning Prayer propers, "Entrance of the Light" in Evening Prayer propers, or the opening sentences in the ordinary of others offices)

[HYMN

(See propers for Morning Prayer, the "Hymn of Light" for Evening Prayer, p. 8, or the ordinary of Compline)

[CONFESSION AND PARDON

(See propers for Evening Prayer or the ordinary of Compline)

INVITATORY AND PSALTER

O Lord, open our lips
And we shall declare your praise.
We praise you, O God.
We praise your holy name!

(See propers for Morning or Evening Prayer
or the ordinary of the hours)

Glory to the blessed and holy Trinity:
One God, now and forever. Amen.

SCRIPTURE(S)

- silence -

CANTICLE

One of the following:
Canticle of Zechariah (*Benedictus*), p. 20
Canticle of Mary (*Magnificat*), p. 10
Canticle of Simeon (*Nunc dimittis*), p. 16
Canticle of Redemption (*De Profundis*), p. 42

29

[AFFIRMATION OF FAITH

PRAYERS
THE LORD'S PRAYER

[COLLECTS (See the ordinary of the hours and the propers for
Morning or Evening Prayer)

[INTERCESSIONS AND THANKSGIVING
(See the propers for Morning or Evening Prayer, the ordinary of
the hours, or The Great Litany)

[PRAYERS OF SPECIAL INTENTION, such as:

A COLLECT FOR THE ORDER OF ST. LUKE
O Shepherd of us all,
who inspired your servant Saint Luke the physician
to set forth in the Gospel the love and healing
power of Jesus:
Grant, we ask you,
your Spirit to the Order of Saint Luke,
that we may proclaim faithfully the Apostolic hope,
magnify the Sacraments,
and bring your healing grace to the whole Church;
Through the same Jesus Christ our Lord. **Amen.**

[HYMN
(See the propers for Morning or Evening Prayer)

DISMISSAL AND GOING FORTH
(See propers for Morning or Evening Prayer
or the ordinary of the hours)

[When celebrated in community, signs of peace may be
exchanged as the community departs.]

THE GREAT LITANY

O God, creator of heaven and earth,
have mercy upon us.

O God, redeemer of the world,
have mercy upon us.

O God, sanctifier of the faithful,
have mercy upon us.

O holy, blessed, and glorious Trinity, one God.
have mercy upon us.

[I]

Remember not, Lord Christ, our offenses, nor the offenses of our forbearers; do not reward us according to our sins. Spare us, good Lord, spare your people whom you have redeemed with your most precious blood; by your mercy preserve us forever.
Spare us, good Lord.

From all evil and wickedness; from sin; from the crafts and assaults of the devil; and from everlasting damnation.
Good Lord, deliver us.

From all blindness of heart; from pride, vainglory, and hypocrisy; from envy, hatred, and malice; and from all want of charity,
Good Lord, deliver us.

From all inordinate and sinful affections;
and from all the deceits of the world, the flesh, and the devil,
Good Lord, deliver us.

From all false doctrine, heresy, and schism;
from hardness of heart, and contempt of your Word and commandment,
Good Lord, deliver us.

From lightning and tempest; from earthquake, fire, and flood;
from plague, pestilence, and famine,
Good Lord, deliver us.
From all oppression, violence, battle, and murder;
and from dying suddenly and unprepared,
Good Lord, deliver us.

By the mystery of your holy incarnation, by your holy nativity,
by your baptism, fasting, and temptation,
Good Lord, deliver us.

By your agony and bloody sweat; by your cross and passion,
by your precious death and burial;
by your glorious resurrection and ascension;
and by the coming of your Holy Spirit,
Good Lord, deliver us.

In all time of our tribulation; in all time of our prosperity;
in the hour of death, and in the day of judgment,
Good Lord, deliver us.

[II]

We beseech you to hear us, Lord God, that your holy church universal might be governed by you in the right way.
We beseech you to hear us, good Lord.

Illumine all bishops, priests and pastors, deacons and ministers, with true knowledge and understanding of your Word;
that both by their speaking and their living,
they may set it forth, and show it accordingly,
We beseech you to hear us, good Lord.

Bless and keep all your people.
We beseech you to hear us, good Lord.

Send forth laborers into your harvest,
and draw all people into your sovereign realm,
> **We beseech you to hear us, good Lord.**

Give to all people increase of grace to hear and receive your Word, and to bring forth the fruits of the Spirit,
> **We beseech you to hear us, good Lord.**

Bring into the way of truth all those who have erred and are deceived,
> **We beseech you to hear us, good Lord.**

Give us a heart to love and fear you,
and to diligently live according to your commandments,
> **We beseech you to hear us, good Lord.**

Rule the hearts of all those in authority that they may do justice and love mercy and walk in the ways of truth.
> **We beseech you to hear us, good Lord.**

Make wars cease in all the world;
give to all nations unity, peace and concord;
and bestow freedom upon all peoples,
> **We beseech you to hear us, good Lord.**

Show pity upon all prisoners and captives, the homeless and the hungry, and all who are desolate and oppressed,
> **We beseech you to hear us, good Lord.**

Preserve the bountiful fruits of the earth,
so that all may enjoy them,
> **We beseech you to hear us, good Lord.**

Inspire us, in our several callings, to do the work you give us to do with singleness of heart as your servants, and for the common good,
> **We beseech you to hear us, good Lord.**

Preserve all who are in danger
by reason of their labor or their travel,
> **We beseech you to hear us, good Lord.**

Preserve and provide for all women in childbirth, young children and orphans, the widows and widowers, and all whose homes are broken or torn by strife,
We beseech you to hear us, good Lord.

Visit the lonely;
strengthen all who suffer in mind, body and spirit;
and comfort with your presence those who are failing and infirm,
We beseech you to hear us, good Lord.
Support, help, and comfort all who are in danger, and tribulation,
We beseech you to hear us, good Lord.

Have mercy upon all people.
We beseech you to hear us, good Lord.

Give us true repentance;
forgive us all our sins, negligence, and ignorance;
and enbue us with the grace of your Holy Spirit to amend our lives according to your holy Word,
We beseech you to hear us, good Lord.

Forgive our enemies, persecutors, and slanderers,
and turn their hearts,
We beseech you to hear us, good Lord.

Strengthen those who stand; comfort and help the weak-hearted; raise up those who fall;
and finally beat down Satan under our feet,
We beseech you to hear us, good Lord.

Grant to all the faithful departed eternal life and peace,
We beseech you to hear us, good Lord.

Grant that in the fellowship of [_____
and] all the saints, we may enter your heavenly realm,
We beseech you to hear us, good Lord.

34

O Lamb of God, who takes away the sins of the world,
have mercy upon us.

O Lamb of God, who takes away the sins of the world,
have mercy upon us.

O Lamb of God who takes away the sins of the world,
grant us your peace.

O Christ hear us:

Kyrie eleison.	or	Lord, have mercy on us.
Christe eleison.		**Christ, have mercy on us.**
Kyrie eleison.		Lord, have mercy on us.

(If the Great Litany is used by itself, it may conclude with
the Lord's Prayer; in an office or eucharistic service, it
concludes with the *Kyrie*.)

[ADAPTED FROM THE 1544 LITANY OF THOMAS CRANMER WHICH WAS BASED ON THE SARUM
ROGATIONTIDE LITANY, LUTHER'S LATIN LITANY OF 1529, AND THE DEACON'S LITANY IN THE
LITURGY OF ST. JOHN CHRYSOSTOM BY DWV]

PROPERS OF THE DAY

FOR

L E N T

COLLECTS and LESSONS
FOR
SAINTS' AND MARTYRS' DAYS

(to replace concluding collects and scripture lessons)

FEBRUARY 24: St. Matthias the Apostle

Almighty God, you chose Matthias to be numbered among the Twelve. Deliver your church from false apostles and give it faithful and true pastors; through your Son Jesus Christ our Lord. **Amen.**

[LUTHERAN BOOK OF WORSHIP, ADAPTED; WPM]

LESSONS
>   Isaiah 66: 1-2
>   Psalm 56
>   Acts 1: 15-26
>   Luke 6: 12-16

MARCH 2: John and Charles Wesley

O almighty God, who in a time of great need raised up your servants John and Charles Wesley, and by your Spirit inspired them to kindle a flame of sacred love which leaped and ran, an inextinguishable blaze: Grant, we ask you, that all those whose hearts have been warmed at these altar fires, being continually refreshed by your grace, may be so devoted that in this our time of great need, your will may fully and effectively be done on earth as it is in heaven; through Jesus Christ our Lord. **Amen.**

[BOOK OF OFFICES AND SERVICES]

LESSONS
>   Isaiah 52: 7-12
>   Psalm 34
>   2 Peter 1: 2-11
>   Mark 12: 28-34

MARCH 19: St. Joseph

O God, who from the family of your servant David raised up Joseph to be the guardian of your incarnate Son and the spouse of his virgin mother: Give us grace to imitate his uprightness of life and his obedience to your commands; through Jesus Christ our Lord, who lives and reigns with you and the Holy Spirit, one God, for ever and ever. **Amen.** [BOOK OF COMMON PRAYER, 239]

LESSONS
>   2 Samuel 7: 4, 8-16
>   Psalm 89: 1-29
>   Romans 4: 13-18
>   Luke 2: 41-52

MARCH 25: The Annunciation

A RESPONSORY:

Today is the beginning of our salvation, and the manifestation of the mystery from the ages;
For the Son of God becomes Son of a virgin.
Therefore, with Gabriel and with Mary, we exult in exceedingly great joy:
For God has regarded the low estate of God's handmaiden
From day to day show forth the salvation of our God.
Sing aloud to God a new song.

[ADAPTED FROM THE TROPARION AND PROKEIMENON OF MATINS FOR ANNUNCIATION DAY IN THE BOOK OF DIVINE PRAYERS AND SERVICES OF THE CATHOLIC ORTHODOX CHURCH OF CHRIST; WPM]

LESSONS
>   Isaiah 52: 7-12
>   Psalm 85 or 87
>   Hebrews 2: 5-10
>   Luke 1: 26-38

COLLECT

Lord God, in the mystery of the incarnation, you chose Mary to bear your Son. Grant that we may show forth the mystery of your love in our lifelong pilgrimage to his cross and resurrection, and so bear Jesus' love to the world; who lives and reigns with you and the Holy Spirit, one God ever. Amen.

[CATHOLIC ORTHODOX CHURCH OF CHRIST; WPM]

EVENING PRAYER FOR THE EVENING BEFORE ASH WEDNESDAY

ENTRANCE OF THE LIGHT
Come, my Light, my Feast, my Strength:
Such a Light, as shows a feast:
Such a Feast, as mends in length:
Such a Strength, as makes us guests.

[FROM GEORGE HERBERT, 1593-1633]

HYMN OF LIGHT (*Phos Hilaron*, see p. 8)

THANKSGIVING FOR THE LIGHT
Our Lord and God:
with your light enlighten the movements of our
meditations that we may hear and understand the
sweet listenings
to your life-giving commands;
and grant that through your grace and mercy
we may gather from them
the assurance of love, and hope, and salvation,
and we shall sing to you everlasting glory
without ceasing and always, O God of all. **Amen.**

[LITURGY OF THE BLESSED APOSTLES, 5TH C.]

EVENING PRAYER CANTICLE (Ps. 141)   (see p. 9)

[INCENSE

CONFESSION AND PARDON
Almighty and eternal God, who drew out a fountain of
living water in the desert for your people, as they well
knew, draw from the hardness of our hearts tears of
compunction, that we may be able to lament our sins,
and receive you in your mercy.

[LATIN, LATE 14TH C.]

39

--silent confession--

If we confess our sins, God is faithful and just, and will forgive our sins and cleanse us from all unrighteousness. **Thanks be to God.**

PSALTER Psalm 36:5-10

SCRIPTURE(S)   Philippians 2:1-13
John 18:15-18, 25-27

-silence-

CANTICLE OF MARY (*Magnificat,* see p. 10, *UMH* 197 st.4 or 198-200)

PRAYERS OF INTERCESSION AND SUPPLICATION
Almighty God, you are rescuer of the lost. When we have cried to you, your steadfast love has brought us to safety and given us a place of rest. For all your mercies to us we give you our most hearty thanks and praise.   [TJC]

Teach us how to rejoice in your salvation.
Teach us to share in your work.

-silent prayer-

Let us pray to God, who knows our needs,
that those who seek strength may find healing . . .
that those who grieve may find comfort . . .
that all the ministers of Christ's holy Church may share the witness of their Lord . . .
Lord, teach us to share you with all people. **Amen.**   [AF]

CONCLUDING COLLECT
O Lord our God, grant us grace to desire you with our whole heart, that so desiring, we may seek and find you, and so finding you we may love you; and loving you we may hate those sins from which you have redeemed us; for the sake of Jesus Christ. **Amen.**   [ST. ANSELM, 1033-1109]

THE LORD'S PRAYER (See *UMH* 270-271 for musical settings)

HYMN   [87.87.87; Tune: *LAUDA ANIMA, UMH* 100]
[This hymn is appropriate as our singing of "alleluia" is put away for Lent]
> Alleluia, song of gladness, voice of joy that cannot die;
> Alleluia is the anthem ever dear to choirs on high;
> In the house of God abiding they lift up their joyful cry.
>
> Alleluia, now resounding, true Jerusalem and free;
> Alleluia, joyful mother, all your children sing with thee;
> But by Babylon's sad waters, mourning exiles we shall be.
>
> Alleluia cannot always be our song while here below;
> Alleluia, our transgressions make us for a while give o'er;
> For the holy time is coming when our tears for sin must flow.
>
> Therefore in our hymns we pray thee, grant us blessed Trinity,
> At the last to keep your Easter, with your saints eternally
> There to you for ever singing Alleluia joyfully.

[ELEVENTH CENTURY LATIN HYMN; J. M. NEALE, TRANS. ALT.]

DISMISSAL AND BLESSING

> We have had feasting and sweetness of milk,
> Honey and water, bread and the cup.
> We have had harp and psaltry and horn,
> Sweet psaltry music and alleluias.
>
> Now the High King of heaven,
> And Jesus the Christ,
> And the Spirit of peace,
> The Spirit of peace and of grace, be with us.
> **Amen and amen!**

[ADAPTED FROM A CELTIC BLESSING ON ASH EVE, DWV]

SENDING FORTH:

> Let us bless the Lord; alleluia!
> **Thanks be to God! Alleluia!!**

(here as silent, symbolic gesture, a banner or scroll with the word
"ALLELUIA" may be put away. We will not sing or hear it again until
we sing it during the Great Paschal Vigil at Easter.)

41

ASH WEDNESDAY VIGIL

CALL TO PRAYER
O Lord, open my lips,
And my mouth shall proclaim your praise.
O God, come to my assistance.
O Lord, hasten to help me.
Glory to you, O Trinity, most holy and blessed:
one God, now and forever. Amen.

CANTICLE OF REDEMPTION (*De Profundis*)
(for a metrical form, see *UMH* 515)

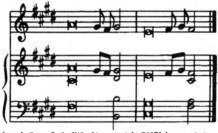

Reprinted from *Lutheran Book of Worship*, copyright ©1978, by permission of Augsburg Fortress

Out of the depths I cry to you, O God;
Lord, <u>hear</u> my voice.
Incline your ear to the voice of my <u>supp</u>lication.

If you were to mark all iniquities,
O God, <u>who</u> could stand?
But there is forgiveness with you
that you <u>may</u> be worshiped.
I wait for the Lord, <u>my</u> soul waits,
and in God's <u>word</u> I hope;
My soul waits for the Lord
more than those who watch <u>for</u> the morning;
more than those who watch <u>for</u> the morning.

O Israel, trust in the Lord;
with God there is mercy and plent<u>eous</u> redemption
for the Lord will redeem Israel from <u>all</u> iniquities.

[PSALM 30; ALT DWV]

THE BLESSING
Lord, grant us your blessing.
May God light the fire of divine love in our hearts.
Amen.

THE PSALTER
[Note: the readings for this office are all taken from the Psalter;
each reading is followed by a time of silence.]

Psalm 5
Psalm 22
Psalm 25 (1-10 in *UMH*)
Psalm 39
Psalm 40 (1-11 in *UMH*)
Psalm 42

CANTICLE OF THE HOLY TRINITY *(Te Deum Laudamus;* see p.18)

COLLECT
Righteous God: In the sacrifice of Christ you show your
love for us. Help us admit to ourselves that have often rejected your love with disdain. Forgive our sin, that
we may reach with confidence for your mercy; through
the same Jesus Christ our Redeemer. **Amen**.   [GLH]

THE LORD'S PRAYER (See *UMH* 270-271 for musical settings)

CONCLUDING PRAYERS
O Lord, hear my prayer,
And let my cry come to you.
Listen to the prayers of your servants;
have mercy on us, Lord Jesus Christ.
Let us bless the Lord.
Thanks be to God!
May the souls of the faithful departed,
through the mercy of God, rest in peace.
Amen.   [ADAPTED FROM THE ROMAN BREVIARY]

MORNING PRAYER
FOR ASH WEDNESDAY

CALL TO PRAYER
> O Lord, open my lips
> **and my mouth shall proclaim your praise.**
> Return to me, says the LORD of hosts,
> and I will return to you. (Zechariah 1:3)

HYMN "Lord, who throughout these forty days" (*UMH* 269)
> *or the following sung to* WAREHAM (*UMH* 260)
>> This fast, as taught by holy lore,
>> We keep in solemn course once more,
>> This Lenten fast is known and bound
>> In forty days each yearly round.
>>
>> In prayer together let us fall
>> And cry for mercy, one and all,
>> And weep before the Judge's feet
>> And God's forgiving love entreat.
>>
>> Your grace have we offended sore
>> By sins, O God, which we deplore;
>> Now pour upon us from on high,
>> O pardoning One, Your clemency.
>>
>> Forgive the sin that we have wrought,
>> Increase the good that we have sought,
>> That we at length, our wanderings o'er,
>> May please You here and evermore.
>>
>> Grant, O most blessed Trinity,
>> Grant, O Essential Unity,
>> That this our fast for forty days
>> May work our profit and Your praise.
>>> [Traditional Daily Office hymn, alt. DTB and DWV]

44

MORNING PRAYER

Almighty and everlasting God: You hate nothing you have made and forgive the sins of all who are penitent. Create in us new and contrite hearts, that we, lamenting our sins and acknowledging our separation, may receive your forgiveness and by your Spirit be renewed in our baptism, through Jesus Christ our Lord. **Amen.**   [BCP ALT]

PSALTER   Psalm 102

SCRIPTURE(S)   Amos 5: 6-15; Hebrews 12: 1-14

--silent reflection--

CANTICLE OF ZECHARIAH (*Benedictus*, see p. 20 or *UMH* 208/209)

PRAYERS OF INTERCESSION AND SUPPLICATION

Purifying Mystery, your light exposes in us all that we hide.
Awaken us and all your Holy Church to spiritual combat.
Lead us to purity of soul and body in these forty days.
Fortify us to take an honest look at our selves and to name our secret sins and our ruts of disobedience.
Let abstinence from our addictions; free us for prayer and the fire of love.
Perfect us by steady gaze toward your pure mercy and grace so we may come to the Passion of Jesus and the Holy Pascha in pure joy.
In confidence we commend ourselves and all our passions and cares to your never failing mercy.

We intercede for the world and the church:
especially for those we have hurt by our preoccupations...
for those who live sacrificially so others may know your justice and compassion...
for a just peace in and among the nations...
for those who help others stand in the light...
for the Church in every place and this congregation...
for the concerns and cares of our lives...   [DTB]

45

CONCLUDING COLLECT
 Holy God, whose spirit drives us into the wilderness to
 confront our priorities with a holy fast; grant that as we
 are   about to do battle with our demons and the power
 of evil, we may be defended by your grace t h r o u g h
 Jesus Christ. **Amen.**   [DTB/DWV]

THE LORD'S PRAYER (See *UMH* 270-271 for musical settings)

HYMN "What Does the Lord Require?" (*UMH* 441 or another
hymn)

DISMISSAL AND BLESSING
 Let us lay aside every weight and the sin that clings so
 closely,
  **and let us run with perseverance the race that is set
  before us, looking to Jesus the pioneer and perfecter
  of our faith.**   [ADAPTED FROM HEBREWS 12: 1-2]
 The grace of the Lord Jesus be with us.
  Thanks be to God. Amen.

EVENING PRAYER
FOR ASH WEDNESDAY

ENTRANCE OF THE LIGHT
 O God, come to our assistance.
  My soul yearns for you in the night.
 Those who sleep in the dust will awake and shout for
 joy;
  for your dew shines forth with sparkling light,
  and the earth will bring those long dead to birth
  again.   (ISAIAH 26:9, 19)

HYMN OF LIGHT (*Phos hilaron*, see p. 8)

46

EVENING PRAYER CANTICLE (Ps. 141)   (see p. 9)

[If not included in some other service on this day, an invitation to the observance of Lenten discipline, a prayer of thanksgiving over the ashes, and the imposition of ashes may be included at this point. See *UMBOW*, pp. 322-323)

CONFESSION AND PARDON

In the dust of isolation and disconnectedness we cry to you, O Lord.
We have loved short-sightedly. We have trusted illusions.
We are left longing and grieving in space that turns from grit and dust, while an angel with whirling sword stands behind us.
Our brows bear the sign of our heart's ashes.
Our life is over like a sigh. In your cross is our only hope.
Come "wash again and ever again this soiled world", through Christ, our only mediator and advocate.
Amen.   [DTB, THE QUOTE IS FROM A LINE OF WALT WHITMAN]

--silence--

"Those who are well have no need of a physician, but those who are sick; I have come to call not the righteous but sinners to repentance."   (Lk 5:31-32)

PSALTER

(Psalm 51 if not used in another service this day or Psalm 90)

--silence--

WORDS OF ASSURANCE

We are touched and healed by the physician of our souls; in the name of Jesus Christ we are forgiven.
Thanks be to God!

SCRIPTURE(S)

--silence--

CANTICLE OF MARY (*Magnificat*, see p. 10, *UMH* 197 st.4, or 198-200)

PRAYERS OF INTERCESSION AND SUPPLICATION

Come, let us enter the inner chamber of our soul,
offering prayers to the Lord and crying aloud:
"Abba in heaven, forgive our sins,
for you alone are truly compassionate."
Enable us to show joyfulness of soul in this fast;
let us not be of sad countenance.
By your Spirit transform our way of life
that we may grow in holiness.

Giving wings to our soul
we offer these prayers to you, Gracious God:
for those who suffer and mourn...
for those who endure patiently the trials of this life...
for the leaders and peoples of your world...
for your church and its mission...
We bless you, O blessed and holy Trinity, uncreated
Unity, the God of all, and exalt you above all forever.
Amen. [ADAPTED FROM ORTHODOX MATINS IN LENT; TAR]

CONCLUDING COLLECT

God of mercy,
who created us from the dust of earth;
and claimed us in Christ through the waters of baptism:
Guide us on our pilgrimage through these desert days
that as a baptized people,
we may hunger and thirst for justice and peace,
and participate in Christ's dying and rising.
May we live and pray in the name of Jesus. **Amen**.

THE LORD'S PRAYER (See *UMH* 270-271 for musical settings)

HYMN [77.77D; Tune:*ABERYSTWYTH, UMH* 479]

Savior, when in dust to thee
Low we bow th' adoring knee;
When, repentant, to the skies
Scarce we lift our weeping eyes;
O by all thy pains and woe
Suffered once for all below,

Bending from thy throne on high,
Hear our solemn litany.
By thy helpless infant years,
By thy life of want and tears,
By thy days of sore distress
In a savage wilderness;
By the dread mysterious hour
Of th' insulting tempter's power:
Turn, O turn a favoring eye,
Hear our solemn litany.

By the sacred griefs that wept
O'er the grave where Lazarus slept;
By the boding tears that flowed
Over Salem's loved abode;
By the mournful word that told
Treach'ry lurked within thy fold:
From thy seat above the sky
Hear our solemn litany.
By thine hour of dire despair;
By thine agony in prayer;
By the Cross, the nail, the thorn,
Piercing spear, and torturing scorn;
By the gloom that veiled the skies
O'er the dreadful Sacrifice:
Listen to our humble cry,
Hear our solemn litany.

By thy deep expiring groan;
By the sad se-pul-chral stone;
By the vault whose dark abode
Held in vain the rising God:
O, from earth to heaven restored,
Mighty, re-ascended Lord,
Listen, listen to the cry
Of our solemn litany.   [SIR R. GRANT, 1785-1838]

GOING FORTH
    May the God of peace
    make you holy in every way
    and keep your whole being--

49

spirit, soul, and body--
free from every fault
at the coming of our Lord Jesus Christ.   (1 Thessalonians 5:23)
Thanks be to God! Amen.

MORNING PRAYER FOR THURSDAYS IN LENT

CALL TO PRAYER
O Lord, open my lips
and my mouth shall proclaim your praise.
Repent and turn from your transgressions.
Get yourselves a new heart and new spirit.
Why will you die?
**I have no pleasure in the death of anyone, says
the Lord God. Turn, then, and live!** (Ezekiel 18:30-32 sel.)

HYMN   [66.66; Tune: *DOLOMITE CHANT, UMH* 455]
I hunger and I thirst;
Jesus, my manna be;
Ye living water, burst
Out of the rock for me.

Thou bruised and broken Bread,
My life-long wants supply;
As living souls are fed,
O feed me, or I die.

Thou true life-giving Vine,
Let me thy sweetness prove;
Renew my life with thine,
Refresh my soul with love.

Rough paths my feet have trod
Since first their course began;
Feed me, thou Bread of God;
Help me, thou Son of Man.

For still the desert lies
My thirsting soul before;
O living waters, rise
Within me evermore. [John Samuel Bewley Monsell, 1811-75]

MORNING PRAYER

Almighty God who sees that we have no power of
ourselves to help ourselves; keep us both outwardly in
our bodies, and inwardly in our souls; that we may be
defended from all adversities which may happen to the
body, and from all evil thoughts which may assault and
hurt the soul; through Jesus Christ our Lord. **Amen.**

[Gregorian Sacramentary]

PSALTER   Psalm 130

SCRIPTURE(S)

--silence--

CANTICLE OF ZECHARIAH (*Benedictus*, see page 20 or *UMH* 208-209)

PRAYERS OF INTERCESSION AND SUPPLICATION

O God our healer and our health,
    we bring our brokenness to you.
Mend what is twisted and paralyzed in us...
Lay your hands upon your Church
    where it is blind and deaf and without voice...
Bend down and write in the dirt before an accused and
        disobedient world...
See with mercy all whose needs and conditions we lift
    before you now...   [DTB]

CONCLUDING COLLECT

Great God, whose Son Jesus came among us to serve:
Teach us the meaning of servanthood. Grant that we
may know when to act and when to show restraint,
when to speak and when to remain silent, so that we may
serve you faithfully and fulfill your purpose for us;
through our Servant Christ. **Amen.**   [GLH]

THE LORD'S PRAYER (See *UMH* 270-271 for musical settings)

HYMN "I Want to Walk as a Child of the Light" (*UMH* 206)

DISMISSAL AND BLESSING
The Lord Jesus Christ be near to defend you, within you
to refresh you, around you to preserve you, before you
to guide you, behind you to justify you, above you to
bless you; who lives and reigns with the Almighty, and
with the Holy Spirit, one God for evermore.

[10TH C. PRAYER, ALT TAR]

Thanks be to God. Amen.

EVENING PRAYER FOR THURSDAYS IN LENT

ENTRANCE OF THE LIGHT
O God, come to our assistance.
O Lord, hasten to help us.
O Israel, hope in God
**with whom there is steadfast love
and plenteous redemption.** (Ps. 130:7)

HYMN OF LIGHT (*Phos hilaron*, see page 8)

[EVENING PRAYER CANTICLE (Ps. 141) (see p. 9)

CONFESSION AND PARDON
O Son of God, who walks among the seven golden
lampstands: the night of sin has covered us. We have
passed our lives in darkness and have returned to our
old selves: hard of heart, anxious in spirit, double
minded in thought and action. So composed we have
sinned against you and our neighbor.

52

--silence for examination of conscience--

[see *UMH* 482-484 for musical settings of the *Kyrie*]
Kyrie eleison.
   Christe eleison.
Kyrie eleison.

--silence--

Forgive us and heal us. Restore us to our right minds and our first love. **Amen.**   [DTB]

PSALTER   Psalm 91

SCRIPTURE(S)

--silence--

CANTICLE OF MARY (*Magnificat*, see p. 10, *UMH* 197 st.4, or 198-200)

PRAYERS OF INTERCESSION AND SUPPLICATION
Let us pray to God who restores our lives and forgives our sins . . .

Let us pray that God will bring health and peace to all who are sick, lonely, grieving or frightened of the challenges for this day . . .

Let us pray that God may restore this earth to its beauty, and create in us hearts that will keep the earth in peace, here, and in all corners of the earth . . .

Let us pray for God to guide our President and all our leaders in the ways of justice and righteousness, to the end that people shall know neither hate, indifference, greed, nor war. . . .

Let us pray for God to fill our Bishop, our superinten-dent, and all ministers, with the Holy Spirit for the work of building the people into God's holy temple . . .

Let us pray to God with thanksgiving, for the good we have known, for the people who have led us to forgiveness, and for those from whom we seek forgiveness . . .

Let us thank God for all the saints of God who have led us to God's own mercy . . .   [AF]

CONCLUDING COLLECT
Grant, Almighty God, that we, who deserve your judgment, by the comfort of your grace may mercifully be relieved; through our Lord and Savior Jesus Christ. **Amen.**   [ADAPTED FROM 1879 BCP; SJM]

THE LORD'S PRAYER (See *UMH* 270-271 from musical settings)

HYMN "O Thou to Whose All-Searching Sight"
> [LM, recommended tune: *TALLIS' CANON, UMH* 682]
> O thou to whose all-searching sight
> The darkness shineth as the light,
> Search, prove my heart; it longs for thee;
> O burst these bonds, and set it free!
>
> Wash out its stains, refine its dross,
> Nail my affections to the cross;
> Hallow each thought; let all within
> Be clean, as thou, my Lord, art clean.
>
> If in this darksome wild I stray,
> Be thou my light, be thou my way;
> No foes, no evils need I fear,
> No harm, while, thou, my God, art near.
>
> Savior, whate'er thy steps I see,
> Dauntless, untired, I follow thee.
> O let thy hand support me still,
> And lead me to thy holy hill!
>   [NICOLAUS L. VON ZINZENDORF 1700-1760; TR. JOHN WESLEY]

GOING FORTH

May the Cross of the Son of God who is mightier than all
the hosts of Satan, and more glorious than all the angels
of heaven, abide with us in our going out and our
coming in! By day and night, at morning and at evening,
at all times and in all places may it protect and defend
us!

From the wrath of evil people, from the assaults of evil
spirits, from the foes invisible, from the snares of the
devil, from all passions that beguile the soul and body,
may it guard, protect, and deliver us.
Thanks be to God! Amen!
[ADAPTED FROM THE *CHRISTARAKANA*, BCP, CHURCH OF INDIA, PAKISTAN, BURMA, AND CEYLON.]

MORNING PRAYER FOR
FRIDAYS IN LENT

CALL TO PRAYER

O Lord, open my lips
and my mouth shall proclaim your praise.
Those who sow with tears
will reap with songs of joy.   [Ps. 126:6; ADAPTED FROM BCP PSALTER]

HYMN "O Love, How Deep, How Broad" (*UMH* 267)

MORNING PRAYER

God who reaches out to us: You have called us to be your
people. Grant that we will have the strength to acknowledge our failure to live in your freedom. Help us to
know that when we turn to you, you are already coming
with joy to welcome us; through Jesus Christ our brother.
Amen.   [GLH]

PSALTER Psalm 6 (or Psalm 105:1-11 in *UMH*)

SCRIPTURE(S)

--silence--

CANTICLE OF ZECHARIAH (*Benedictus,* see p 20 or *UMH* 208, 209)

PRAYERS OF INTERCESSION AND SUPPLICATION
We bless and praise and magnify you, O God of mercy.
You have led us out of the shadows of night once more
into the light of day. To your loving-kindness we make
our entreaty:
  be merciful to us in our misdeeds;
  accept our prayers in the fullness of your compassions,
    for you are our refuge from one generation to
    another.
We await the Day of justice and reconciliation when all
enter the gates of the new Jerusalem and feast at your
heavenly banquet. Until that day, cause us to discern
that many have not yet entered your banquet hall.
Instead of lapsing into bad manners by beginning to
feast while you are still looking for the missing guests,
prompt us to prayerful search for the countless millions
in the world who languish in suffering, injustice, hun
ger, war, isolation and abuse. With eyes and hearts open
to the empty places at the table, we pray:
  for youth who long for life...
  for refugees and exiles...
  for all who suffer and are in trouble...
  for leaders who have power for good and evil...
  for the Church sleeping in the light...
  for those people and concerns that arise in the silence
  now...   [ADAPTED FROM A GREEK PRAYER; DTB]

CONCLUDING COLLECT
Suffer the true Sun of your Righteousness to shine in
our hearts; enlighten our reason, and purify our
senses; that we may walk honestly as in the day, in
the way of your commandments, and reach at last
the life eternal, where we shall rejoice in your Life,
and in your Light shall we see light. **Amen.**   [DTB]

THE LORD'S PRAYER (See *UMH* 270-271 for musical settings)

HYMN   [LM; tune: *GERMANY, UMH* 415]
   O Sun of Righteousness, we pray
   Our darkened minds may know thy day,
   That healing light may shine once more
   As day to earth Thou dost restore.

   While praying in this time apart,
   Oh, grant us, now a contrite heart
   And may by kindness those be turned
   Who long Thy patient love have spurned.

   That day draws nigh, Thy saving hour
   When all things made anew shall flow'r;
   Oh, let us greet with joyful face
   That day which brings us back Thy grace.

   May all creation worship Thee,
   O blessed, holy Trinity,
   And we, by mercy now restored,
   May sing a new song to the Lord.
                [ADAPTED FROM A TRADITIONAL DAILY OFFICE HYMN, DTB, DWV]

DISMISSAL AND BLESSING
   May the eternal God bless and keep us, guard our
   bodies, save our souls, direct our thoughts, and
   bring us safe to our eternal home, where the ever
   blessed Trinity lives and reigns, one God for ever
   and ever.   [SARUM BREVIARY ALT]
   Thanks be to God! Amen.

EVENING PRAYER FOR FRIDAYS IN LENT

ENTRANCE OF THE LIGHT
O God, come to our assistance.
 O Lord, hasten to help us.
As Moses lifted up the serpent in the wilderness,
so must the Son of Man be lifted up,
that whoever believes in him may have eternal life.

[JOHN 3:14-15]

HYMN OF LIGHT   (*Phos hilaron,* see page 8)

[EVENING PRAYER CANTICLE (Ps. 141)   (see p. 9)

CONFESSION AND PARDON
O God, whose nature and property is ever to have mercy
and to forgive, receive our humble petitions...

--silence--

Though we be tied and bound with the chain of our sins,
yet may the pity of your great mercy loose us...
--silence--
O Lord Jesus Christ, who gave your life for us that we
might receive pardon and peace; mercifully cleanse us
from all sin, and evermore keep us in your favor and
love, who lives and reigns with the Almighty and the
Holy Spirit, ever one God, world without end. **Amen..**

[ADAPTED FROM 6TH C. PRAYERS OF GREGORY THE GREAT AND AN ANCIENT COLLECT; TAR]

In Jesus Christ, we are forgiven.
 Thanks be to God!

PSALTER   Psalm 115 (1-11 in *UMH*)

SCRIPTURE(S)
--silence--

58

CANTICLE OF MARY (*Magnificat*, see p. 9, UMH 197 st.4, or 198-200)

PRAYERS OF INTERCESSION AND SUPPLICATION

Let us pray through Christ our Lord; by his birth and his life, by his words and his sufferings, by his death on the Cross and his resurrection from the dead.

Let us pray for the sick and the recovering, the lost and the found, for our friends and our enemies . . .

Let us pray for those who suffer from illness and disease, for the homeless and those in prison . . .

Let us pray that God will make us strong in prosperity and give us wisdom in calamity so that when we are put to the test, we may not fall aside . . .

Let us pray for God to illumine our President, all national rulers and governments. Through the Holy Spirit, let there be peace on earth . . .

Let us pray for God to guide and bless the Church throughout the world, in all its ministries; that we may grow in unity, faith and love . . .

Let us pray for God to lead us in the ways of justice; that all may have their proper share of God's good gifts, and know the presence of Christ's love . . .   [ADAPTED AF]

CONCLUDING COLLECT

We pray to you, uncreated and eternal God.
Hold out your hand to us and help us to our feet.
Merciful God, pull us upward.
Give us the courage to stand up without shame or guilt.
Revoke the death sentence against us
and write our names in the book of life
with all your holy prophets and apostles. **Amen.**

[SERAPION OF THUMIS, FOURTH CENTURY]

THE LORD'S PRAYER (See *UMH* 270-271 from musical settings)

HYMN "Blessed Jesus at Thy Word" *(UMH* 596)

GOING FORTH

The God of peace, who brought again from the dead our Lord Jesus, that great shepherd of sheep, through the blood of the everlasting covenant, make us perfect in every good work to do God's will, working in us that which is well-pleasing in God's sight; through Jesus Christ, to whom be glory for ever and ever. (HEBREWS 13: 20, 21)

Thanks be to God! Amen.

Mary Magdalene Grieving
(from a French Renaissance sculpture of Christ's entombment)
©C. E. Visminas
reprinted from *And Also With You: Year A*
©1992 OSL Publications
by permission

MORNING PRAYER FOR SATURDAYS IN LENT

CALL TO PRAYER
O Lord, open my lips
and my mouth shall proclaim your praise.
Store up for yourselves treasures in heaven, where
neither moth nor rust consumes. (Mt. 6:23)

HYMN   [LM; Tune: *ROCKINGHAM, UMH* 299]

Ho! Everyone that thirsts, draw nigh,
Come to the living waters, come!
Mercy and free salvation buy;
Return ye weary wanderers, home.

See from the rock a fountain rise!
For you in healing streams it rolls,
Money you need not bring, nor price,
O laboring, burdened, sin-sick souls.

Why seek ye that which is not bread,
Nor can your hungry souls sustain?
On ashes, husks, and air you feed;
And spend your little all in vain.

I bid you all my goodness prove;
My promises for all are free;
Come, taste the manna of my love,
And let your soul delight in me.

[CHARLES WESLEY]

MORNING PRAYER
O God of Light, Creator of Life, Giver of Wisdom,
Benefactor of our souls, giving to the fainthearted who
put their trust in you those things into which the angels
desire to look; O Sovereign, who has brought us up from

61

the depths of darkness to light, who has given us life from death, who has graciously bestowed upon us freedom from slavery, and who has scattered the darkness of sin within us; now also enlighten the eyes of our understanding, and sanctify us wholly in soul, body, and spirit. **Amen.** [ADAPTED FROM THE LITURGY OF ST. MARK, 3RD C.; TAR]

PSALTER   Psalm 19

SCRIPTURE(S)

--silence--

CANTICLE OF ZECHARIAH (*Benedictus*, see page 20; or *UMH* 208-209)

PRAYERS OF INTERCESSION AND SUPPLICATION
Let us pray for the people of Christ's Church throughout the world, for all ministers of the Gospel; for all teachers and leaders that all may be good stewards of God's grace.

. . .

Let us pray for Christian missions everywhere; for those who care for the unemployed, for those who teach, for those who heal the injured body and soul, and those who provide nourishment and hope.

. . .

Let us pray that justice, truth, and love may prevail in our world, that there may be no more war, and that all people may live together in harmony; guide our President, the Congress, and all rulers to the end that there may be peace.

. . .

Let us pray for all children, and especially those of our families and churches, that they may grow into faithful witnesses of Jesus Christ.

. . .

Let us pray for all who are suffering from sickness of body or mind, especially - - - ; for those who draw near to the end of life; for the hungry, the imprisoned, and the lonely. Let us pray for God's healing to be upon all people in need. . .

[ADAPTED FROM BOW 1966, AF]

CONCLUDING COLLECT

O God, who is the unsearchable abyss of peace, the ineffable sea of love, the fountain of blessings, and the bestower of affection; open to us today the sea of your love, and water us with the plenteous streams from the riches of your grace. Enkindle in us the fire of your love; sow in us your fear; strengthen our weakness by your power; bind us closely to you and to each other in one firm bond of unity; for the sake of Jesus Christ. **Amen.**

[ADAPTED FROM SYRIAN CLEMENTINE LITURGY, 1ST C.; TAR]

THE LORD'S PRAYER (See *UMH* 270-271 for musical settings)

HYMN [Tune: *DOLOMITE CHANT, UMH* 455]

My spirit longs for thee
Within my troubled breast,
Though I unworthy be
Of so divine a guest.

Of so divine a guest
Unworthy though I be,
Yet has my heart no rest
Unless it comes from thee.

Unless it come from thee,
In vain I look around;
In all that I can see
No rest is to be found.

No rest is to be found
But in thy bless-ed love:
O let my wish be crowned,
And send it from above.

[J. BYROM, 1691-1763]

GOING FORTH

May the Lord bless us with all good and keep us from all evil; may God give light to our hearts with loving wisdom, and be gracious to us with eternal knowledge; may God's loving countenance be lifted upon us for eternal peace.

Thanks be to God. Amen.　　　[ADAPTED FROM DEAD SEA SCROLLS; TAR]

EVENING PRAYER FOR SATURDAYS IN LENT

ENTRANCE OF THE LIGHT
> O God, come to our assistance.
> **O Lord, hasten to help us.**
> Send out your light and your truth;
> let them lead us. (Ps. 43:3)

HYMN OF LIGHT (*Phos hilaron,* see page 8)

THANKSGIVING FOR THE LIGHT
> O Light of the World, we give thanks for your love which can never cease, that kindles our lamps but does not extinguish them: may they may burn in us and enlighten others.

> O Christ, our dearest Savior, kindle our lamps, that they may evermore shine in your temple, that we may receive unquenchable light from you that will enlighten our darkness, and lessen the darkness of the world. Lord Jesus, we pray, give your light to our lamps, that in its light we may always behold you, desire you, look upon you in love, and long after you, for your sake. **Amen.** [ADAPTED FROM COLUMBA, 6TH C.; TAR]

[EVENING PRAYER CANTICLE (Ps. 141)   (see p. 9)

CONFESSION AND PARDON
> O Lamb of God, we have forgotten our baptismal profession in our daily life:
> > we have embraced incompatible loyalties,
> > we have not linked baptism with martyrdom.
> > we have let theology and liturgy be diversions
> > > rather than calls to faithfulness.
> O Christ, renew the love and courage we had at first.

Bring us down from the towers of speculation and
out from caves of inwardness to loyalty in the world
where your passion still calls us to resist evil and share
in your victory of love.
Jesus, forgive our sin and heal our will.

--silence for examination of conscience--

"He saved us, not because of any works of righteousness
that we had done, but according to his mercy through the
water of rebirth and renewal of the Holy Spirit." (Titus 3:5)
In the name of Jesus Christ we are forgiven and called.

[DTB]

Thanks be to God!

PSALTER   Psalm 43

SCRIPTURE(S)

--silence--

CANTICLE OF MARY (*Magnificat*, see p. 10, *UMH* 197 st.4, or 198-200)

PRAYERS OF INTERCESSION AND SUPPLICATION

In peace, we pray to you, Lord God:
For all people in their daily life and work . . .
For our families, friends, and for those who are alone . . .
For this community, the nation, and the world . . .
For all who work for justice, freedom and peace . . .
For the just and proper use of your creation . . .
For the victims of hunger, fear, injustice, and oppression . . .
For all who are in danger, sorrow, or any kind of trouble . . .
For those who minister to the sick, the friendless,
   and the needy . . .
For the peace and unity of the Church of God . . .
For all who proclaim the Gospel,
   and all who seek the truth . . .

Lord, let your loving-kindness be upon us
for we put our trust in you. [BCP, Form VI]

CONCLUDING COLLECT

Accept the evening thanksgiving of your baptized
people, O Fountain of all good. You have led us safely
through the length of the day; you daily bless us with so
many mercies, and you have given us the hope of
resurrection to eternal life; through Jesus Christ our
Lord. **Amen.** [ADAPTED FROM 5TH C. COLLECT; TAR]

THE LORD'S PRAYER (See *UMH* 270-271 for musical settings)

HYMN [LM; Tune: *HURSLEY, UMH* 616]

Creator of the world, give ear,
with gracious love our prayers to hear,
prayers which our longing spirits raise
who keep this Lent of forty days.

Each heart is open unto thee;
thou knowest our infirmities.
Now we repent, give us thy grace,
that we may each thy love embrace.

Spare us, O God; we now confess
our sins and seek your holiness
that for the glory of thy Name,
our sin-sick souls may health regain.

Grant, blessed, holy Trinity,
One God, eternal Unity;
that baptized by thy grace and blessed
we may bear fruit of holiness.
[*AUDI, BENIGNE CONDITOR*; ATR TO GREGORY THE GREAT, 540-604, DWV]

GOING FORTH

May God bless us with all heavenly benediction, and
make us pure and holy by divine perception. May the

riches of God's glory abound in us. May God instruct us
with the word of truth, inform us with the Gospel of
salvation, and enrich us with love, Through Jesus Christ,
our Lord.
Thanks be to God! Amen.

[ADAPTED FROM GELASIAN SACRAMENTARY; TAR]

MORNING PRAYER FOR SUNDAYS IN LENT

CALL TO PRAYER
O Lord, open my lips
and my mouth shall proclaim your praise.
All I want is to know Christ and the power of his
resurrection and the sharing of his sufferings by becom-
ing like him in his death. (PHILIPPIANS 3:10)

HYMN   [SM; Tune: *ST. MICHAEL, UMH* 372]

Jesus, we follow Thee,
In all Thy footsteps tread,
And pant for full conformity
To our exalted Head.

We in Thy birth are born,
Sustain Thy grief and loss,
Share in Thy want, and shame, and scorn.
And die upon Thy cross.

Baptized into Thy death
We sink into Thy grave,
Till Thou the quickening Spirit breathe,
And to the utmost save.

Thou said'st, 'Where'er I am
There shall My servant be;
Master, the welcome word we claim
And die to live with Thee.

[No. 130 OF WESLEY'S HYMNS ON THE LORD'S SUPPER]

67

MORNING PRAYER

O God of strength, passing all understanding, who mercifully gives to your people mercy and judgment; grant that we may faithfully love you, and walk today in the way of righteousness; through Jesus Christ our Lord. **Amen.** [SARUM BREVIARY, 11TH C. ALT]

PSALTER   Psalm 28

SCRIPTURE(S)

--silence--

CANTICLE OF ZECHARIAH (*Benedictus*, see page 20; or *UMH* 208-209)

PRAYERS OF INTERCESSION AND SUPPLICATION

Risen Christ, even in Lent we celebrate your resurrection each Lord's day. As your baptized people, we yearn to share more fully in the paschal mystery which has marked our lives with the sign of the cross. Hear us as we pray:

for insight into the implications of our discipleship . . .
for courage to set our face toward our Jerusalems . . .
for compassion to meet the needs of others . . .
for grace to overwhelm our lack of faith . . .
for faithfulness in what is entrusted to us . . .

We lift up your church around the world this day. Cleanse, reform and empower it so that we may be channels of your love and justice.

Especially we lift up: . . . [DWV]

CONCLUDING COLLECT

Almighty God, who fills all things with your presence, we humbly ask you, of your great love, to keep us near to you today; grant that in all our ways and doings we may remember that you see us, and may always have grace to know and perceive what things you would have us to do, and strength to fulfill the same; through Jesus Christ our Lord. **Amen.** [ADAPTED FROM 5TH C. COLLECT; TAR]

THE LORD'S PRAYER (See *UMH* 270-271 for musical settings)

HYMN "Father, We Thank You" (*UMH* 565)

GOING FORTH
The God of peace brought our Lord Jesus, the great shepherd of the flock, back from the dead. May God give us every good gift, that we may do God's will. May God work within us all that is pleasing in God's sight through Jesus Christ. (HEBREWS 13: 20, 21)
Thanks be to God! Amen.

EVENING PRAYER FOR SUNDAYS IN LENT

ENTRANCE OF THE LIGHT
O God, come to our assistance.
O Lord, hasten to help us.
May those who sow in tears reap with shouts of joy.
(Ps. 126:5)

HYMN OF LIGHT (*Phos hilaron,* see page 8)

THANKSGIVING FOR THE LIGHT
Thanks be to you, O Lord,
the Light, the Way, the Truth, the Life;
in you there is no darkness, or death.
You are the Light without which there is darkness;
the Way without which there is wandering;
the Truth without which there is error;
the Life without which there is Death.

Lord, say: "let there be Light,"
and I shall see Light, and eschew Darkness;
I shall see the Way and avoid wandering;
I shall see the Truth and shun error;
I shall see Life and escape Death.

Illuminate, O illuminate my soul
which sits in darkness and the shadow of Death;
and direct my feet into the way of peace. **Amen.**

[AUGUSTINE, 4TH C. ALT]

[EVENING PRAYER CANTICLE (Ps. 141) (see p. 9)

CONFESSION AND PARDON

O Lord, who gave to your Apostles peace, shed down upon us all your holy calm; gather together with your hand all those who are scattered, and bring them like sheep into the fold of your holy Church, through Jesus Christ our Lord.

Strengthen and confirm me, O Lord, by your Cross, on the rock of faith, that my mind be not shaken by the attacks of the Enemy. For you alone are holy.

You know, O Lord, how many and great are my sins, you know how often I sin, from day to day, from hour to hour, in the things I do and the things I leave undone. No more, O Lord, no more, O Lord my God, will I provoke you; no more shall my desire be for anything but you, for you alone are truly lovable.
And if again I offend in anything, I humbly ask you of your mercy to grant me strength to find favor again in your sight and to live in a manner more pleasing to you.

--silence--

"This saying is sure and worthy of full acceptance, that Christ Jesus came into the world to save sinners." "If any one sins, we have an advocate with God, Jesus Christ the righteous; and he is the expiation for our sins, and not for ours only but also for the sins of the whole world."
Thanks be to God.

[CONFESSION ADAPTED FROM THEODORE STUDITA, 8TH C.; TAR
PARDON FROM I TIMOTHY 1:15 AND I JOHN 2:1-2]

PSALTER   Psalm 126

SCRIPTURE(S)

--silence--

CANTICLE OF MARY (*Magnificat*, see p. 10, *UMH* 197 st.4, or 198-200)

PRAYERS OF INTERCESSION AND SUPPLICATION:

A BIDDING PRAYER

In silence, pray that all God's children may be brought together in unity to offer God thanksgiving, praise and love.

. . . . .

In community, pray for the world, that we may use the earth's resources to care for one another; that prisoners may receive proper care; and that each person may be preserved in dignity.

. . . . .

In hope, pray for our nation, our President and the leaders of earthly governments; inspire them with peace, that we may be delivered from the threat of war and injustice.

. . . . .

In compassion, pray for all who suffer in body, mind, or spirit, remembering especially (those named here and in our hearts); give each one courage and hope in their troubles, and bring them the joy of your salvation.

. . . . .

In faith, pray for the Church, for _____ our Bishop, and _____, our Superintendent, for all pastors and all who serve Jesus Christ in his Church.

. . . . .

Commend to God's care all those who have departed this life, and pray that we may so live in faith and love so as share with all God's saints in eternal life.

. . . . .   [AF]

CONCLUDING COLLECT

Sacrificial God whose gift of love was rejected by people like ourselves: Work in us such true remorse that we may accept your grace, receive your mercy, and live in wonder; praising the perfect sacrifice of the Savior through whom we pray. **Amen.**   [GLH]

THE LORD'S PRAYER (See *UMH* 270-271 for musical settings)

HYMN
[77.77; Tune: *CANTERBURY, UMH* 355]

Forty days and forty nights
You were fasting in the wild;
Forty days and forty nights
Tempted and yet undefiled:

Sunbeams scorching all the day;
Chilly dew-drops nightly shed;
Prowling beasts about the way;
Stones your pillow, earth your bed.

And if Satan, vexing sore,
Flesh or spirit should assail,
You, his vanquisher before,
Grant we may not faint nor fail.

So shall we have peace divine;
Holier gladness ours shall be;
Round us too shall angels shine,
Such as ministered to thee.

Keep, O keep us, Savior dear,
Ever constant by thy side;
That with thee we may appear
At the eternal Eastertide.

[G.H. SMYTTAN, 1822-1870 AND F. POTT, 1832-1909]

GOING FORTH
May the God of hope fill you with all joy and peace in believing, so that you may abound in hope by the power of the Holy Spirit.   (Romans 15:13)
Thanks be to God. Amen.

MORNING PRAYER FOR MONDAYS IN LENT

CALL TO PRAYER
  O Lord, open my lips
  and my mouth shall declare your praise.
  While he was still far off, his father saw him and was
  filled with compassion; he ran and put his arms
  around him and kissed him.   (Lk. 15:20)

HYMN "Come, Ye Sinners, Poor and Needy" (*UMH* 340)
  or "Where Shall My Wondering Soul Begin" (*UMH* 342)

MORNING PRAYER
  All-knowing God: You know that in this world we are
  under great pressure. At times we cannot stand. Grant
  that we may stiffen our resolve by your mercy. Make
  our faith strong, so that we may overcome temptation;
  through Jesus Christ, the source of our strength. **Amen.**
                                                [GLH]

PSALTER Psalm 32

SCRIPTURE(S)
                    --*silence*--

CANTICLE OF ZECHARIAH (*Benedictus,*see page 20 or *UMH* 208-209)

PRAYERS OF INTERCESSION AND SUPPLICATION
  Cover us, Lord, with your mercy;
  restrain us from the misuse of money, power, and sex.
  Give us a passion for your reign of compassion and
  justice and the will to love you in all the small duties of
  this day.
  Restore us to the grace and dignity of our baptism
  and remind us that our work is priestly service.
  As those who live touching another world,
  we bring you this one:
    the holy church on the front lines of martyrdom
      and congregations blinded by trifles...

the nations ravaged by contests of power and misuse
of wealth and creation's gifts...
those who suffer: the unemployed, the betrayed,
the desperate and depressed...
the needs and cares which rise up in us
by your Spirit's sighing...   [DTB]

CONCLUDING COLLECT
O One whose glory is revealed through Jesus to his
followers: Help us to hear your word and perceive the
wonder of divine love. Enable us to grow in grace so that
we will descend from the mountain with Christ to the
sick and wanting world below; we pray through Christ
our Savior. **Amen.**   [GLH]

THE LORD'S PRAYER (See *UMH* 270-271 for musical settings)

HYMN "Guide Me, O Thou Great Jehovah" (*UMH* 127)

GOING FORTH
Righteousness and justice are the foundation of your
throne;
steadfast love and faithfulness go before you.   (Ps. 89:14)
Thanks be to God! Amen!

EVENING PRAYER FOR MONDAYS IN LENT

ENTRANCE OF THE LIGHT (as lamps are lighted)
Light and peace in Jesus Christ, our Lord.
Thanks be to God.
Wondrously show your steadfast love,
O savior of those who seek refuge
from their adversaries at your right hand.   (Ps. 17:7)

HYMN OF LIGHT (*Phos hilaron*, see page 8)

[EVENING PRAYER CANTICLE (Ps. 141)   (see p. 9)

CONFESSION AND PARDON
God of covenant and grace: you have called us in baptism to be bearers of the Light but we have fallen into the darkness of pride. Like Lucifer, we have wanted to be the Light, full of earthly power and grandeur, revered and praised for our greatness. We have wanted the way of success and the way of magic and ease.

Forgive us when and where we have not been the Light bearers today:
in jostling for attention...
in protecting our position...
in deceptive speech...
in noise that trumpeted our agenda...
In silence now we yield the excesses of our desire and pride to the true light, Jesus Christ.

-a time of silence: letting go and letting Jesus look upon us-

"Let this same mind be in you that was in Christ Jesus,
who, did not regard equality with God
as something to be exploited,
but emptied himself, taking the form of a slave
being born in human likeness."   (PHILIPPIANS 2: 5-7)
**In the name of Jesus Christ we are forgiven
and restored to the Light.**   [DTB]

PSALTER   Psalm 17

SCRIPTURE(S)
--silence--

CANTICLE OF MARY (*Magnificat,* see p. 10, *UMH* 197 st.4, or 198-200)

PRAYERS OF INTERCESSION AND SUPPLICATION
We beg you, Lord,
to help and defend us.

Deliver the oppressed . . .
Pity the insignificant . . .
Raise the fallen . . .
Show yourself to the needy . . .
Heal the sick . . .
Bring back those of your people who have gone astray . . .
Feed the hungry . . .
Lift up the weak . . .
Take off the prisoner's chains . . .

May every nation come to know that you alone are God,
    that Jesus Christ is your child,
    that we are your people, the sheep of your pasture.

[CLEMENT OF ROME, LATE 1ST CENTURY; DTB]

CONCLUDING COLLECT

We humbly pray, O Father in Heaven, to guide us through the darkness of this world, to guard us from its perils, to hold us up and strengthen us when we grow weary in our mortal way; and to lead us by your chosen paths, through time and death, to our eternal home in your heavenly kingdom through Jesus Christ our Lord. **Amen.**

[ADAPTED FROM KING'S CHAPEL LITURGY, 1831; DTB]

THE LORD'S PRAYER (See *UMH* 270-271 for musical settings)

HYMN   [LM; Tune: *THE GIFT OF LOVE, UMH* 408]

O Christ, you are the Light and Day,
'Fore whom the darkness flees away,
You, "very Light of Light," we own,
Who has your glorious light made known.

All-holy Lord, to you we bend;
Your servants through this night defend;
Oh, grant us calm and quiet night,
Then wake us to your morning light.

Asleep though weary eyes may be,
Still keep our hearts awake to Thee,
Let your right hand outstretched above
Guard those who serve the Lord they love.

Look down, O Lord, our strong Defense;
Repress our foes' proud insolence;
Preserve and govern us for good--
Whom you have purchased with your blood.

Remember us, dear Lord, we pray,
Within this mortal frame of clay;
For you alone our souls defend;
Be with us, Savior, to the end.

All laud to God eternally;
All praise, eternal Christ to Thee,
Whom with the Spirit we adore,
Forever and forevermore.

[CHRISTE, QUI LUX ES ET DIES; AN AMBROSIAN HYMN; TRANS. W. J. COPELAND, 1848; ALT DWV]

GOING FORTH
O Israel, hope in GOD,
With whom there is steadfast love,
and great power to redeem.
It is God who will redeem Israel from all iniquities.

(ADAPTED FROM PS. 130:7-8)

Thanks be to God! Amen.

MORNING PRAYER FOR TUESDAYS IN LENT

CALL TO PRAYER
O Lord, open my lips
and my mouth shall proclaim your praise.
"O Lord, look at my affliction,
for the enemy has triumphed"

(LAMENTATIONS 1:9)

HYMN   "O Love, How Deep" (*UMH* 267)

MORNING PRAYER

> Jesus, we confess you, our Savior, Messiah, Priest and
>   Lord.
> For us you did all things well.
> For us you intercede in love and liberation
>   at the right hand of God.
> For us you discipline our affections and loyalties
>   so we may be healed.
> Cheer us as you lead us through the desert
>   of these forty days. **Amen..**   [DTB]

PSALTER   Psalm 137 (1-6)

SCRIPTURE(S)

> *--silence--*

CANTICLEOFZECHARIAH(*Benedictus,*seepage20;orUMH208-209)

PRAYERS OF INTERCESSION AND SUPPLICATION

> Lord God, whom we love and whom we desire to love
> more, bring us to love you as much as we ought.
> Come with Christ and dwell in our hearts and keep
> watch over our lips, our steps, our deeds and we shall
> not need to be anxious either for our souls or our bodies.
> Give us love that knows no enemy and love that is for
> others as you love us.
> Cause our hearts frozen in sin, cold to you and cold to
> others, to be warmed by your divine fire.
>
> [ADAPTATION OF A PRAYER OF ST. ANSELM, DTB]

> Hear us as we embrace in the circle of your love:
>   the life of your church...
>   the world groaning...
>   the cares of our own lives...
>   and those particular concerns which your Spirit
>   prompts within us...   [DTB]

CONCLUDING COLLECT

Living and dying, Lord, we would be yours;
keep us yours forever,
and draw us day by day nearer to yourself,
until we are wholly filled with your love
and fitted to behold you, face to face. **Amen.**

[ADAPTED FROM A PRAYER BY EDWARD BOUVERIE PUSEY; DTB]

THE LORD'S PRAYER (See *UMH* 270-271 for musical settings)

HYMN "By Gracious Powers" (*UMH* 517)

GOING FORTH

Blessed be the God and Father of our Lord Jesus Christ,
the Father of mercies and the God of all consolation, who
consoles us in all our affliction so we may be able to
console those who are in any affliction.

(2 CORINTHIANS 1:3-4)

Thanks be to God! Amen.

EVENING PRAYER FOR TUESDAYS IN LENT

ENTRANCE OF THE LIGHT

O God, come to our assistance.
O Lord, hasten to help us.
Wait for God; be strong and let your heart take courage.

(PS. 27:14)

HYMN OF LIGHT (The *Phos hilaron*, see page 8)

[EVENING PRAYER CANTICLE (Ps. 141) (see p. 9)

CONFESSION AND PARDON

O God, pardon our offenses,
done voluntarily or involuntarily, wittingly, or
unwittingly,

79

by word or deed or in thought;
forgive those that are hidden and those that are
  manifest,
those which were done long ago,
those which are known, and those which are forgotten,
  but are known to you.
Forgive us, O God, through Jesus Christ our Lord.
Amen.   [FROM THE LITURGY OF SYRIAN JACOBITES]

--silence--

If you, O God, should mark iniquities,
  LORD, who could stand?
But there is forgiveness with you,
  so that you may be worshipped.   (Ps. 130:3-4)
    Thanks be to God!

PSALTER   Psalm 27

SCRIPTURE(S)

--silence--

CANTICLE OF MARY (*Magnificat*, see p. 10, *UMH* 197 st.4, or 198-200)

PRAYERS OF INTERCESSION AND SUPPLICATION
    God who nurtures us — God of power without end:
    Hear our prayers, answering them as you deem best for us.
    We pray for the church catholic; that we may glimpse
      the hope of Jerusalem . . .
    For all who in self-righteousness criticize the actions of
      others without attempting to understand them . . .
    For those who request prayer or for whom prayer has
      been requested, that they may experience your heal
      ing . . .
    For those we name before you in our hearts, that they
      may know the power of your love . . .
    For ourselves, that we, receiving your Word with open
      hearts, may embrace your promise, heed your com-
      mands, and declare your praise . . .

80

CONCLUDING COLLECT
God our Savior and Redeemer: you are constantly at work, reaching out to us in every circumstance. Hear the prayers we make to you, and continue to bring forth new things in your creation; through Jesus Christ our Sovereign. **Amen.** [GLH]

THE LORD'S PRAYER (See *UMH* 270-271 for musical settings)

HYMN "Out of the Depths" (*UMH* 515)

GOING FORTH
The blessing of the Lord rest and remain upon all God's people, in every land, of every tongue; the Lord meet in mercy all that seek God; the Lord comfort all who suffer and mourn; the Lord hasten the coming glory, and give us, God's people, the blessing of peace.

[ADAPTED FROM BISHOP HANDLEY MOULE, 1841-1920; TAR]

Thanks be to God. Amen.

MORNING PRAYER FOR WEDNESDAYS IN LENT

CALL TO PRAYER
O Lord, open my lips
and my mouth shall proclaim your praise.
God be merciful to me, a sinner. (LK. 18:13)

HYMN [LM; Tune: *GERMANY, UMH* 427]

O God of morning and of night,
We thank you for your gifts of light;
As in the dawn the shadows fly,
We seem to find you now more nigh.

Fresh hopes have wakened in the heart,
Fresh force to do our daily part;
In peaceful sleep our strength restored
Throughout the day to serve you more.

O God of light, your love alone
Can make our human hearts your own;
Be ever with us, Christ, that we
May faithful, baptized people be.

[FRANCIS TURNER PALGRAVE 1824-1897, ALT DWV]

MORNING PRAYER

Write your blessed name, O Lord, upon my heart,
there to remain so indelibly engraved,
that no prosperity, no adversity
shall ever move me from your love.

Be to me a strong tower of defense,
a comforter in tribulation,
a deliverer in distress,
a very present help in trouble,
and a guide to heaven
through the many temptations and dangers of this
life. **Amen.**   [THOMAS Á KEMPIS, 15TH C.]

PSALTER   Psalm 143

SCRIPTURE(S)

--silence--

CANTICLE OF ZECHARIAH (*Benedictus*, see page 20; or *UMH* 208-209)

PRAYERS OF INTERCESSION AND SUPPLICATION
(The Great Litany; introductory prayer to God and part I or II,
see page 31)

CONCLUDING COLLECT

God of holy love: You offer living water to the world
through Jesus. Keep us close to Christ, that our thirst for
righteousness may be quenched unto eternal life; through
the Source of our salvation. **Amen.**   [GLH]

THE LORD'S PRAYER (See *UMH* 270-271 for musical settings)

HYMN "Take Up Thy Cross" (*UMH* 415)

GOING FORTH
The time is fulfilled, and the kingdom of God has come near; repent, and believe in the good news.   (Mark 1:15)
We believe; Lord, help our unbelief!
The grace of the Lord Jesus Christ and the love of God and the *koinonia* of the Holy Spirit is with us now and always!
Thanks be to God! Amen.

EVENING PRAYER FOR WEDNESDAYS IN LENT

ENTRANCE OF THE LIGHT
O God, come to our assistance.
O Lord, hasten to help us.
Behold, now is the acceptable time,
behold, now is the day of salvation.   (2 Corinthians 6:2)
The Son of Man came not to be served but to serve, and to give his life as a ransom for many.

(Mark 10:45)

HYMN OF LIGHT (*Phos hilaron,* see page 8)

[EVENING PRAYER CANTICLE (Ps. 141)   (see p. 9)

CONFESSION AND PARDON
God of mercy and judgement who calls us to fast and pray:
We confess the ingratitude of our hearts
and all the ways we try to improve upon the life you give us-
   -our complicating simple gifts
   -our impatience with grace unfolding

-our demanding of life on our terms
-our lack of hospitality for unexpected visitations
and surprises.
We repent of our lack of trust and gratitude. Give us
grace to fast from hurry and discover the immense
simplicity of things through Jesus Christ our Lord.

--silence--

"Listen! I am standing at the door knocking; if you
hear my voice and open the door, I will come into
you and eat with you, and you with me." (REVELATION 3:20)

**We are forgiven and released from captivity.
Thanks be to God!**

[DTB]

PSALTER   Psalm 103

SCRIPTURE(S)

--silence--

CANTICLE OF MARY (*Magnificat,* see p. 10, *UMH* 197 st. 4 or 198-200)

PRAYERS OF INTERCESSION AND SUPPLICATION
God of the covenant, we give you thanks this day that
we are numbered among your sons and daughters.
Through Christ you made us as numerous as the stars
of the sky, and by your Spirit you empower us for your
work.

We pray this day for those who are tempted to give
up hope in your promise . . .
For the sick in mind, body, or spirit, that they may be
succored by the knowledge of your Presence . . .
For all outcasts and those without home or land, that
a place of refuge, shelter, and belonging will soon
be theirs . . .
For all who lead the nations, that, relying not upon
their own strength, they may lift their minds above
the things of earth and focus upon the things of
heaven . . .

Grant that we in your Church may be responsible citizens of your heavenly country. Forbid that we should become so familiar with the call of Christ that we ignore His claim upon our lives. Shape our endeavors to coincide with your desires. As you lead us toward the land you have promised, send forth your Spirit to guide us on our journey. May what we do be cause for rejoicing, and who we are reflect your radiance; we pray through Jesus Christ the author of our faith. **Amen.**   [GLH]

CONCLUDING COLLECT
Thanks be to you, O Lord Jesus Christ,
for all the benefits which you have given us;
for all the pains and insults which you have borne for us.

O most merciful Redeemer, friend and brother,
may we know you more clearly,
love you more dearly,
and follow you more nearly, for your own sake.
Amen.   [Richard of Chichester, 13th c.]

THE LORD'S PRAYER (See *UMH* 270-271 for musical settings)

HYMN "Thy Holy Wings, O Savior" (*UMH* 502)

GOING FORTH
May God in the plenitude of love
pour upon you torrents of grace,
bless you and keep you in holy fear,
open to you the paschal mystery,
and receive you at last into eternal glory.
Thanks be to God! Amen.
[Adapted Blessing from the Consecration of Coventry Cathedral; TAR; DWV]

MORNING PRAYER FOR PALM/PASSION SUNDAY

CALL TO PRAYER
> O Lord, open my lips
> **and my mouth shall proclaim your praise.**
> Lift up your heads, O gates! and be lifted up, O
> ancient doors! that the King of glory may come in.

(Ps. 24:7)

HYMN   [LM; Tune: *THE KING'S MAJESTY, BOH* 425]

> Ride on! Ride on in majesty!
> Hark! all the tribes Hosanna cry;
> O Savior meek, pursue Thy road
> With palms and scattered garments strowed.
>
> Ride on! Ride on in majesty!
> In lowly pomp ride on to die:
> O Christ, Thy triumphs now begin
> O'er captive death and conquered sin.
>
> Ride on! Ride on in majesty!
> The winged squadrons of the sky
> Look down with sad and wondering eyes
> To see the approaching sacrifice.
>
> Ride on! Ride on in majesty!
> In lowly pomp ride on to die;
> Bow Thy meek head to mortal pain,
> Then take, O God, Thy pow'r and reign.

[HENRY HART MILMAN, 1791-1868]

MORNING PRAYER
> God whose Christ was given to be the Savior of your people:
> As he courageously entered Jerusalem, grant that we may
> with boldness and faith proclaim your salvation to all;
> through the same Jesus our Redeemer. **Amen..**   [GLH]

PSALTER   Psalm 118: 19-29

SCRIPTURE   Zechariah 9: 9-12 and/or:
            Year A: Mt. 21: 1-11
            Year B: Mk. 11: 1-10
            Year C: Lk. 19: 28-40

                        -silence-

CANTICLE The *Sanctus*
        Let us bless the Lord with praises and loud shouts
        of thanksgiving:
                (see musical settings *UMH* 19-28)
        Holy, holy, holy Lord, God of power and might,
        heaven and earth are full of your glory.
            Hosanna in the highest.
        Blessed is the one who comes in the name of the
        Lord.
            Hosanna in the highest!

PRAYERS OF INTERCESSION AND SUPPLICATION
        We praise you, Almighty God, for the acts of love by
        which you have redeemed us through your Son Jesus
        Christ our Lord, who, on this day entered the holy city
        of Jerusalem in triumph, and was proclaimed as king by
        those who spread their garments and branches of palm
        along his way. We too celebrate Christ's triumphal
        entry into the city by lifting our voices in praise and by
        laying our prayers at your feet. Especially today we
        pray:
            for those who stand aside, silently suspicious of you...
            for the children who cry "Hosanna," when we will
                not listen...
            for those who seek to silence your word and work...
            for those who have long awaited your coming glory...
            for those who need your healing presence...
                                    [ADAPTED FROM BCP; TAR]

CONCLUDING COLLECT

Everlasting God, who presented Jesus to be welcomed as Messiah on the way to the cross: enable us who have been clothed with Christ's grace in baptism to spread ourselves like coats under his feet and bear witness to his reign in the world. **Amen.**

[BASED ON A LINE FROM ANDREW OF CRETE, 8TH C.; DTB]

THE LORD'S PRAYER

HYMN "At the Name of Jesus" (*UMH* 168)

DISMISSAL AND BLESSING

It is ourselves that we must spread under Christ's feet, not coats or lifeless branches or shoots of trees, matter which wastes away and delights the eye only for a few brief hours. But we have clothed ourselves with Christ's grace, and with the whole Christ--"for as many of you as were baptized into Christ have put on Christ"-- so let us spread ourselves like coats under his feet.

**Like splendid palm branches,
we are strewn in the Lord's path.**

[ANDREW OF CRETE, 8TH C.; LATIN ANTIPHON]

EVENING PRAYER FOR PALM/PASSION SUNDAY

ENTRANCE OF THE LIGHT

O God, come to our assistance.
O Lord, hasten to help us.
Blessed is the one who comes in the name of the Lord!
The Lord is God who has given us light.

(PSALM 118:26-27 SEL)

HYMN OF LIGHT (*Phos hilaron*, see page 8)

88

THANKSGIVING FOR THE LIGHT

Eternal God, uncreated and primal Light, Maker of all created things, Fountain of pity, Sea of Bounty, fathomless deep of Loving-Kindness: lift up the light of your countenance upon us! Shine in our hearts, true Sun of Righteousness, and fill our souls with your beauty.

Teach us always to keep in mind your teachings, to talk together about them, and own you continually as our Lord and Friend. Govern by your will the works of our hands; and lead us in the right way, that we may do what is well-pleasing and acceptable to you, that through us your holy name may be glorified. To you alone be praise and honor and worship eternally. **Amen.**   [BASIL; 4TH C. ALT]

[EVENING PRAYER CANTICLE (Ps. 141) (see p. 9)

CONFESSION AND PARDON

O Lord of life and truth, hear our confession and transform us with your terrible mercy. We are diminished because we have not been truthful that sin deals death to the world. We have done evil before you and to the poor, the innocent and the powerless. We have done our own will and not yours. We have been only half-hearted in keeping our appointments with you. Because of our poor discipleship, the Church fails to be a visible embodiment of Jesus and his love. Renew in us crucified love and restore us to your Church as a living sign of your reign.   [DTB]

--silence for the examination of conscience--

The Lord is God who has given us light.
Lead the festal procession with branches,
    up to the horns of the altar!
O give thanks to the Lord who is good,
    for God's steadfast love endures for ever!

(PS. 118:27, 29; ADAPTED)

Thanks be to God.

PSALTER Psalm 103

SCRIPTURE Zechariah 12: 9-11; 13:1, 7-9

--silence--

CANTICLE OF MARY (*Magnificat,* see page 10, *UMH* 197 st. 4, or 198-200)

PRAYERS OF INTERCESSION AND SUPPLICATION
O God whose Son set his face toward Jerusalem: As he did not turn from the cross, grant that we will not shrink from our duty as your messengers. Prepare us to take up the cross, that we may truly be disciples of our Savior; the same Jesus Christ our Lord.

Hear our prayers for:
for our friends and family...
for those who feed the hungry, house the homeless, clothe the naked, and visit the imprisoned...
for those deprived of dignity...
for people confined by disability or illness...
for those who wrestle with doubt or despair...
for those confronting the mystery of death...
for the church's ministries of compassion...
for new beginnings in our lives...
for our call to discipleship with Christ...

CONCLUDING COLLECT and THE LORD'S PRAYER
O God, compose our spirits to a quiet and steady dependence on thy good providence. Help us to set a watch before our mouths and keep the door of our lips. And let not our hearts incline to any evil thing or to practice wicked works with those who work iniquity. But as we have received how we ought to walk and to please thee, so may we abound more and more. Protect us, we beseech thee, and all our friends everywhere this night, and awaken in the morning those good thoughts in our hearts, that the words of our Savior may abide in us and we in him, who taught us when we pray to say:
Our Father...

[ADAPTED FROM JOHN WESLEY; TAR]

HYMN

O thou, from whom all goodness flows,
I lift my heart to thee;
In all my sorrows, conflicts, woes,
Good Lord, remember me.

When on my aching burdened heart
My sins lie heavily,
Thy pardon grant, thy peace impart:
Good Lord, remember me.

When trials sore obstruct my way,
And ills I cannot flee,
Then let my strength be as my day:
Good Lord, remember me.

If worn with pain, disease, and grief
This feeble spirit be,
Grant patience, rest, and kind relief:
Good Lord, remember me.

And O, when in the hour of death
I bow to thy decree,
Jesus, receive my parting breath:
Good Lord, remember me.   [T. Haweis, 1734-1820]

GOING FORTH

Passing from one divine feast to another,
from palms and branches,
let us now hasten, O faithful,
to the solemn and saving celebration of Christ's passion.
Let us behold him undergo voluntary suffering for our sake,
and let us lift up our voices to him with thanksgiving:
   **Fountain of tender mercy and haven of salvation,
   O Lord, glory to you!**

[Byzantine Vespers]

MORNING PRAYER FOR MONDAY OF HOLY WEEK

CALL TO PRAYER
Answer me, O Lord, for your love is kind;
in your great compassion turn to me.

(Ps. 69:18, BCP)

HYMN   "Hope of the World"   (*UMH* 178)

MORNING PRAYER
Lord our God, holy is your name!
Incline our hearts to you
and give us the wisdom of the cross,
so that, freed from sin,
which imprisons us in our own self-centeredness,
we may be open to the gift of your Spirit,
and so become living temples of your love.
Amen.   [ITALIAN SACRAMENTARY]

PSALTER Psalm 36: 5-10

SCRIPTURE(S)
        Year A: Mt. 21: 12-17
        Year B: Mk. 11: 15-19
        Year C: Lk. 19: 45-48

--silence--

CANTICLE OF ZECHARIAH (*Benedictus,* see p. 20 or *UMH* 208-209)

PRAYERS OF INTERCESSION AND SUPPLICATION
We humble ourselves, O Lord of heaven and earth, before thy glorious majesty. We acknowledge thy eternal power, wisdom, goodness, and truth, and desire to render unto thee most unfeigned thanks for all the benefits which thou pourest upon us, and above all, for thine inestimable love in the redemption of the world by our Lord Jesus Christ.

Let us abound in thy love more and more, and in
continual prayers and praises to thee, the Lord of
mercies and God of all consolation...

And we desire the good of all humanity, especially of
all Christian people, that they may walk worthy of
the gospel and live together in unity and Christian love...

Bless all those that watch over souls; direct their
labors and give us grace to follow their godly admo
nitions...

The same blessings we crave for our friends, relations,
and acquaintances, that we may all live in perfect love
and peace together, and rejoice together at the great day
of the Lord Jesus...   [ADAPTED FROM JOHN WESLEY; TAR]

CONCLUDING COLLECT

God of Righteousness: Cleanse your church of impiety,
reveal our sinfulness, and enable us to be a holy people who
are always ready to proclaim your mighty acts; by the
merits of the One who died offering life to all. **Amen.**

[GLH]

THE LORD'S PRAYER

HYMN   [66.66.888; Tune: *RHOSYMEDRE, UMH* 447]

My song is love unknown,
My Savior's love to me,
Love to the loveless shown,
That they might lovely be.
O who am I, that for my sake
My Lord should take frail flesh, and die?
My Lord should take frail flesh, and die?

He came from his blest throne,
Salvation to bestow;
We turned away and none
The longed-for Christ would know.
But O, my Friend, my Friend indeed,
Who at my need his life did spend!
Who at my need his life did spend!

Sometimes they strew his way,
And his sweet praises sing;
Resounding all the day
Hosannas to their King.
Then 'Crucify!' is all their breath,
And for his death they thirst and cry.
And for his death they thirst and cry.

Why, what has my Lord done?
What makes this rage and spite?
He made the lame to run,
He gave the blind their sight.
Sweet injuries! Yet they at these
Themselves displease, and 'gainst him rise.
Themselves displease, and 'gainst him rise.

They rise, and needs will have
My dear Lord made away;
A murderer they save,
The Prince of Life they slay.
Yet cheerful he to suffering goes,
That he his foes from thence might free.
That he his foes from thence might free.

In life, no house, no home
My Lord on earth might have;
In death, no friendly tomb
But what a stranger gave.
What may I say? Heaven was his home;
But mine the tomb wherein he lay.
But mine the tomb wherein he lay.

Here might I stay and sing.
No story so divine;
Never was love, dear King,
Never was grief like thine!
This is my Friend, in whose sweet praise
I all my days could gladly spend.
I all my days could gladly spend.

[S. CROSSMAN, 1624-1683]

DISMISSAL AND BLESSING

Now that you have purified your souls by your obedience to the truth so that you have a genuine mutual love, love one another deeply from the heart. You have been born anew. (1 PETER 1:22-23)

Thanks be to God.

EVENING PRAYER FOR MONDAY OF HOLY WEEK

ENTRANCE OF THE LIGHT

O God, come to our assistance.
O Lord, hasten to help us.
The Lord is my light and my salvation, whom shall I fear?
The Lord is the stronghold of my life;
of whom shall I be afraid? (Ps. 27:1)

HYMN OF LIGHT (*Phos hilaron*, see page 8)

[EVENING PRAYER CANTICLE (Ps. 141) (see page 9)

CONFESSION AND PARDON

O God, who teaches us your saving word, enlighten our souls with the comprehension of the things which have been before spoken to us, so that we may not only be hearers of the word, but also doers of good d e e d s , striving after guileless faith, blameless life, and pure conversation.

Release, pardon, and forgive, O God, all our voluntary and involuntary sins, which we commit in action and in word, knowingly and ignorantly, by night and by day, in mind and thought. Forgive us all in goodness and love.

Sanctify, O Lord, our souls, bodies and spirits; examine our minds and search our consciences; take from us all evil imaginations, all impurity of thought, all inclinations to lust, all depravity of conception, all envy, pride and hypocrisy, all falsehood, deceit and irregular living, all covetousness, vain glory and sloth; all malice, anger and wrath, all remembrance of injuries, all blasphemy and every motion of flesh and spirit that is contrary to the purity of your will.   [LITURGY OF ST. JAMES, 2ND C.]

--silence--

The saying is sure and worthy of full acceptance, that Christ Jesus came into the world to save sinners. If any one sins, we have an advocate with the Father, Jesus Christ the righteous; and he is the expiation for our sins, and not for ours only but also for the sins of the whole world.
   Thanks be to God.

PSALTER   Psalm 27:1-6

SCRIPTURE LESSON
          Year A: Mt. 21: 33-46
          Year B: Mk. 12: 1-12
          Year C: Lk. 20: 9-19

--silence--

CANTICLE OF MARY (*Magnificat,* see p. 10, *UMH* 197, st. 4; 198-200)

PRAYERS OF INTERCESSION AND SUPPLICATION
          Hear our prayer, O Lord;
             Listen to our cry.
          You shall arise and have mercy on Zion,
             For the time of Zion's favor has come.

God forbid that I should glory, save in the Cross of
our Lord Jesus Christ.

**In him is salvation, life, and resurrection from
the dead.**

By him we are redeemed and set at liberty.

**God be merciful to us, and bless us, and shine
your divine countenance upon us.**

[ADAPTED FROM *SERVICE BOOK AND HYMNAL*; WPM]

CONCLUDING COLLECT

O God, most merciful, who in the beginning created us,
and by the passion of your only begotten Son has created
us anew, work in us now, we pray, both to will and to
do your good pleasure. And as much as we are weak,
and can do no good thing of ourselves, grant us your
grace and heavenly benediction, that in whatever work
we engage we may do all to your honor and glory; and
that, being kept from sin and daily increasing in good
works, so long as we live in the body we may ever show
forth some service to you; and after our departure may
receive pardon of all our sins, and attain eternal life;
through Christ who, with you and the Holy Ghost, lives
and reigns for ever and ever. **Amen.**

[ADAPTED FROM ANSELM, 11TH C.; TAR]

THE LORD'S PRAYER

HYMN "Depth of Mercy" (*UMH* 355)

GOING FORTH

The Lord bless us and keep us.
The Lord be kind and gracious to us.
The Lord look upon us with favor
and give us peace.

(NUMBERS 6:24-26; ALT)

Thanks be to God. Amen.

97

MORNING PRAYER FOR TUESDAY OF HOLY WEEK

CALL TO PRAYER
Answer me, O Lord, for your love is kind;
in your great compassion turn to me.

(Ps. 69:18, BCP)

HYMN   "O Love That Wilt Not Let Me Go" (*UMH* 480)

MORNING PRAYER
God whose mercy knows no limits: As your divine Word
reached out to humanity, grant that we, the   be-lieving
people of Christ, will share our knowledge of salvation;
through Jesus Christ our Savior. **Amen.**   [GLH]

PSALTER   Psalm 71:1-6

SCRIPTURE LESSON
            Year A: Mt. 22: 23-33
            Year B: Mk. 12: 18-27
            Year C: Lk. 20: 27-40

--silence--

CANTICLE OF ZECHARIAH (*Benedictus*, see p. 20 or *UMH* 209)

PRAYERS OF INTERCESSION AND SUPPLICATION
Not only our ancestors alone did the Holy One redeem
but us as well, along with them, as it is written: "And
God freed us from Egypt." Therefore, let us rejoice at the
wonder of our deliverance: from bondage to freedom,
from agony to joy, from mourning to festivity, from
darkness to light, from servitude to redemption.
We pray for your deliverance, O God:
    for those who remain in spiritual and emotional bondage...
    for those who long for your joy...

for those who suffer and mourn...
for those who languish in the darkness of loneliness
and depression...
for all who are in need of your redemption...
Prepare us, O God, to sing a new song.

[ADAPTED FROM *The Passover Haggadah*; TAR]

CONCLUDING COLLECT

O God, whose blessed Son, for the redemption of the world did ascend the cross, that your wisdom might enlighten the whole world: Pour that same light, we pray, into our souls and bodies, that we might come into your light eternal; Through the same Jesus Christ our Lord, who with you and the Holy Spirit lives and reigns, one God, forever and ever. **Amen.**

THE LORD'S PRAYER

HYMN [LM; Tune: *OLIVE'S BROW, UMH* 282]

Lord, Jesus, when we stand afar,
And gaze upon thy holy Cross,
In love of thee and scorn of self,
O may we count the world as loss!

When we behold your bleeding wounds,
And the rough way that you have trod,
Make us to hate the load of sin
That lays so heavy on our God.

O holy Lord, uplifted high,
With outstretched arms, in mortal woe,
Embracing in your wondrous love
The sinful world that lies below,

Give us an ever-living faith,
To gaze beyond the things we see;
And in the mystery of your death
Draw us and all now unto thee.

[BISHOP W. WALSHAM HOW, 1823-1897]

DISMISSAL AND BLESSING
    May the God of peace
    make us holy in every way
    and keep our whole being--
    spirit, soul, and body--
    free from every fault
    at the coming of our Lord Jesus Christ.

(1 Thessalonians 5:23)

    Thanks be to God. Amen.

EVENING PRAYER FOR TUESDAY OF HOLY WEEK

ENTRANCE OF THE LIGHT
    O God, come to our assistance.
    O Lord, hasten to help us.
    Let us take refuge in you,
        and let us never be put to shame.   (Ps. 71:1)

HYMN OF LIGHT (*Phos hilaron*, see page 8)

[EVENING PRAYER CANTICLE (Ps. 141)   (see page 9)

CONFESSION AND PARDON
    Turn away, O Lord, the fierceness of your wrath,
    and in pity spare your people:
        Lord, have mercy.
        O Christ, look upon our groanings,
    loose the bands of death, and grant us life:
        Christ, have mercy.
    Behold our tears — consider our sighs,
    and in pity forgive our sins:
        Lord, have mercy.

--silence--

100

O Lord, if you marked iniquities, Lord, who could stand? But there is forgiveness with you, that you may be feared. **Amen.**.

[CONFESSION FROM MOZARABIC BREVIARY, 7TH C.; ALT; PARDON FROM PSALM 130: 3-4]

PSALTER   Psalm 71: 7-12

SCRIPTURE LESSON
>   Year A: Mt. 24: 1-8
>   Year B: Mk. 13: 1-8
>   Year C: Lk. 21: 5-11

--silence--

CANTICLE OF MARY (*Magnificat*, see p. 10, *UMH* 197 st. 4, or 198-200)

PRAYERS OF INTERCESSION AND SUPPLICATION
O God, from the time we were in our mothers' wombs, you have been the One on whom we have leaned. Our praises are continually of you. As our days pass, you remain steadfast as our strong fortress and refuge. We sing the greatness of your holy Name from of old.

Fill us with the power of your Holy Spirit that we who are weak may boast of the Lord. Enkindle in us the light of the knowledge of how you have come to save all of creation and give us the strength to proclaim your greatness to the ends of the earth; assist us to bring the powerful to worship before your throne.

There are among our concerns this day those who would see Jesus. Many are in danger of losing their lives to disease; others suffer greatly because they cannot understand the world around them; persecution lies heavy on the heads of people we love. Visit them in your mercy, O God, and deliver them from their distress.

You have glorified your Name, almighty God, and you will glorify it again. Give us a spirit of glory as you hear and answer us as we pray in the name of Jesus. **Amen.**

[*AND ALSO WITH YOU: A*; TJC; SEL]

CONCLUDING COLLECT

Eternal God, grant me true quietness,
For you are rest and quiet without end.
Eternal light, grant me the abiding light,
That I may live and quicken in your good. **Amen.**

[ANGILBERT, 8TH C.]

THE LORD'S PRAYER

HYMN [CM; Tune: *CAMPMEETING, UMH* 492]

All you who seek for sure relief
In trouble and distress,
Whatever sorrow vex the mind,
Or guilt the soul oppress,

Jesus, who gave himself for you
Upon the Cross to die,
Opens to you his sacred heart:
O to that heart draw nigh.

You hear how kindly he invites;
You hear his words so blest:
'All you that labor come to me,
And I will give you rest.'

O Jesus, joy of saints on high,
O hope of sinners here,
Attracted by those loving words
To you we lift our prayer.

Wash thou our wounds in that dear Blood
Which from your heart does flow;
A new and contrite heart on all
Who cry to you bestow. [18TH C. TR. E. CASWALL]

GOING FORTH

May the God of hope fill you with all joy and
peace in believing, so that you may abound in
hope by the power of the Holy Spirit.

(ROMANS 5: 13)

Thanks be to God. Amen.

MORNING PRAYER FOR WEDNESDAY OF HOLY WEEK

CALL TO PRAYER
    Answer me, O Lord, for your love is kind;
    in your great compassion turn to me.   (Ps. 69:18, BCP)

HYMN   [CM; Tune: *CRIMOND, UMH* 118]
    My God, I love you, not because
    I hope for heaven thereby,
    Nor yet because who love you not
    Are lost eternally.

    You, O my Jesus, you did me
    Upon the Cross embrace;
    For me did bear the nails and spear,
    And manifold disgrace,

    And griefs and torments numberless,
    And sweat of agony;
    Yea, death itself — and all for me
    Who was your enemy.

    Then why, O bless-ed Jesus Christ,
    Should I not love you well?
    Not for the sake of winning heaven,
    Nor of escaping hell;

    Not from the hope of gaining aught,
    Nor seeking a reward;
    But as yourself has lov-ed me,
    O ever-loving Lord.

    So would I love you, dearest Lord,
    And in your praise will sing;
    Solely because you are my God,
    And my most loving King. [17TH C. TR. E CASWALL; ALT DWV]

MORNING PRAYER

O God, who for our redemption gave your only be-
gotten Son to the death of the Cross, and by his glorious
resurrection delivered us from the power of the enemy.
Grant us so to live our baptism that we may die daily to
sin, and evermore live with you, in the joy of the
resurrection; through the same Jesus Christ our Lord.
Amen.   [ADAPTED FROM GREGORY THE GREAT; TAR]

PSALTER   Psalm 69: 1-8 (*BCP*)

SCRIPTURE LESSON
          Year A: Mt. 26: 6-13
          Year B: Mk. 14: 3-9
          Year C: Jn. 12: 1-8

--silence--

CANTICLE OF ZECHARIAH (*Benedictus,* see p. 20 or *UMH* 208-9)

PRAYERS OF INTERCESSION AND SUPPLICATION

O God, all who seek you find their cause for rejoicing and
are glad in you. Holy and blessed is your Name.
In spite of your abiding mercy and deliverance we seek to
withhold that which belongs to you. We follow our own
ways and fall subject to the ways of evil so that we, too,
betray you. When confronted with the ways we fall short of
your will, we look for others on whom to put the blame.
Your words are clear, but we fail to understand. In your
covenant faithfulness you have called us to lay aside our sin.
O Lord, you are our help and our deliverer. Have mercy
upon us. Come quickly and forgive our sin.

The cloud of witnesses which surrounds us is filled with
your Holy Spirit. So, too, fill us this day with that same
Spirit that we may lay aside every burden and run the
race that is set before us with joy, that all the world may
know that mercy lies in you.

We lift up before you this day many who have grown weary and fainthearted because they have been struck down by illness of body, mind, or spirit. We know you have compassion for them because you have endured assaults on every side. Reach out to these and grant them peace and deliverance from suffering.

O God, deliver us all, for the sake of Him who is the pioneer and perfecter of our faith, even Jesus Christ, your Son our Lord, in whose holy Name we pray. **Amen.** [AND ALSO WITH YOU:A; TJC ALT]

CONCLUDING PRAYER

God the Deliverer of Israel: As your Anointed freed us from captivity to sin and death by your mighty power, empower us to work for the liberation of all people; by the merits of Christ our Emancipator. **Amen.** [GLH]

THE LORD'S PRAYER

HYMN "Be Still, My Soul" (*UMH* 534)

GOING FORTH

God forbid that I should glory, save in the Cross of our Lord Jesus Christ.
In him is salvation, life, and resurrection from the dead.
God be merciful to us, and bless us, and shine your divine countenance upon us. [ADAPTED FROM SCRIPTURE; WPM]
Thanks be to God. Amen.

EVENING PRAYER FOR WEDNESDAY OF HOLY WEEK

ENTRANCE OF THE LIGHT
O God, come to our assistance.
O Lord, hasten to help us.
Unless a grain of wheat falls into the earth and dies, it remains alone; but if it dies, it bears much fruit.

(JOHN 12:24)

HYMN OF LIGHT (*Phos hilaron*, see page 8)

[EVENING PRAYER CANTICLE (Ps. 141) (see page 9)

CONFESSION AND PARDON
O God, the Son of God — so loving, yet hated — so forbearing, yet assaulted unto death — who showed yourself merciful to your persecutors; grant that through the wounds of your passion our sins may be forgiven, and as in your humiliation you suffered death for us, so now, being glorified, bestow on us everlasting brightness.

--silence for confession--

We who once were estranged and hostile in mind, doing evil deeds, Christ has now reconciled in his body of flesh by his death, in order to present us holy and blameless and irreproachable before God.
Thanks be to God.

[CONFESSION: MOZARABIC LITURGY, 7TH C.; PARDON: COLOSSIANS 1:21-22]

PSALTER   Psalm 70

SCRIPTURE
Year A: Mt. 26: 1-5, 14-16
Year B: Mk. 14: 1-2, 10-11
Year C: Lk. 22: 1-6

--silence--

CANTICLE OF MARY (*Magnificat*, see p. 10, *UMH* 197 st.4, or 198-200)

PRAYERS OF INTERCESSION AND SUPPLICATION
Save us, O God, and raise us up by your Christ.

Let us beg for the mercies of the Lord, and for God's
compassion ...
for the angel of peace ...
for those things which are good ...
for a Christian departure out of this life ...
for an evening and a night of peace, and free from sin ...
and let us beg that the whole course of our life
glorify our Savior Jesus Christ.

O Living God, we dedicate ourselves and one another
to you through Christ our Lord. **Amen.**

[ADAPTED FROM APOSTOLIC CONSTITUTIONS, 4TH C.; TAR]

CONCLUDING COLLECT
God of mercy: look down, we beseech you, Lord, on
your family, for whose sake our Lord Jesus Christ did
not hesitate to be betrayed into the hands of the wicked
and to undergo the torment of the cross and renew us by
your Spirit in these holy days that we might serve you
faithfully, through the same Jesus Christ our Lord.
Amen.   [ROMAN RITE; ALT DWV]

THE LORD'S PRAYER

HYMN "My Faith Looks Up to Thee" (*UMH* 452)

GOING FORTH
The Lord Jesus Christ be near to defend us, within to
refresh us, around to preserve us, before to guide us,
behind to justify us, above to bless us; who lives and
reigns with you and the Holy Spirit, one God for evermore.
Thanks be to God. Amen.   [ANONYMOUS, 10TH C.]

107

MORNING PRAYER FOR THURSDAY OF HOLY WEEK

CALL TO PRAYER
The firstfruits of the Lord's Passion fill this present day with light. Come then, all who love to keep the feast, and let us welcome it with songs.
For the Creator draws near to undergo the cross.
[BYZANTINE MATINS]
"Where is my guest room where I may eat the Passover with my disciples?" (Mark 14:14)

HYMN "Jesus, Priceless Treasure" (*UMH* 532)

MORNING PRAYER
Jesus, our feet are dirty from the journey. How will we become clean again? When evening comes, who will make us clean and ready for the meal? Where will we find the water for these soiled soles? Restore us to the joy of God's salvation. **Amen..** [DTB]

PSALTER   Psalm 102

SCRIPTURE LESSON
         Year A: Mt. 26: 17-19
         Year B: Mk. 14: 12-16
         Year C: Lk. 22: 7-13

--silence--

CANTICLE OF ZECHARIAH (*Benedictus*, see page 20 or *UMH* 209)

PRAYERS OF INTERCESSION AND SUPPLICATION
God our provider, you feed us with the bread of life and lift for us the cup of salvation, and all we have is from your generous love in Jesus Christ. We praise you for every blessing of life in his name. Especially we thank you:

108

for the loyalty of friends...
for the love of families...
for worship shared with your people in the church...
for the mystery of life itself...
God our redeemer, you invite all to your feast, but
not all can taste of life's joys. We remember before
you, therefore, those in special need. Especially we pray:
for those who feel unwanted or unloved...
for people alone and forgotten...
for the dying and those who wait with them...
for those imprisoned...
for Christians who suffer in the service of Christ...

[*DAILY PRAYER*, PCUSA]

CONCLUDING COLLECT

O Lord of desert and solitude, O Mystery transforming:
we come to the end of these forty days that bring profit
to our souls: plunge us now into the mystery of your
passion and bring us to the triumph of holy Easter as,
by your grace, we pass over from death to life and from
sin to the glorious liberty of the daughters and sons of
God. **Amen.** [DTB]

THE LORD'S PRAYER

HYMN "For the Bread Which You Have Broken"

(*UMH* 614 or 615)

DISMISSAL AND BLESSING

Christ our passover is sacrificed for us.
Therefore, let us keep the feast.
Thanks be to God. Amen.

TRIDUUM

Since the fourth century, the Church has observed the holy *triduum* (the great three days) of the crucified, buried, and risen Lord. It is the central point of the liturgical year, beginning on Holy Thursday evening, reaching its climax in the Great Vigil of Easter, and closing with Paschal Vespers on Easter Sunday.

The church observes these days in a variety of ways. Some congregations come closer to the pattern of the Daily Office during the Triduum than at any other time of the church year. Some of these offices will be replaced by the observances of the congregation of which one is a part. Never-the-less, because few parishes observe all of the Triduum, resources are provided for all of the offices.

Some of these will become "solitary" offices supplementary to the "people's services" or "cathedral offices" of the congregation. Others may be used or adapted by churches for "prayer vigils." A gathered community may choose to observe the complete cycle as it participates in the paschal mystery celebrated by the Triduum.

EVENING PRAYER FOR HOLY THURSDAY

ENTRANCE OF THE LIGHT
 The Love of Christ has gathered us as one.
 Let us rejoice and be glad in him.
 Let us fear and love the living God,
 and in purity of heart let us love one another.
 Where charity and love are, there is God.
 When therefore we are gathered together
 let us not be divided in spirit.
 Let bitter strife and discord cease between us;
 Let Christ our God be present in our midst.
 Where charity and love are, there is God.
 With all the blessed may we see forever
 your face in glory, Jesus Christ our God.
 Joy that is infinite and undefiled
 for all the ages of eternity.
 Where charity and love are, there is God.

 [MAUNDY THURSDAY, WESTERN RITE]

HYMN OF LIGHT (*Phos hilaron*, see page 8)

[INCENSE

[EVENING PRAYER CANTICLE (Ps. 141)   (see page 9)

CONFESSION AND ASSURANCE
 The *Kyrie* (For musical settings, see *UMH* 482-484)
  Lord, have mercy.
  Christ have mercy.
  Lord, have mercy.

 Psalm 51

--silence--

Assurance:
If we confess our sins, God is faithful and just, and will forgive our sins and cleanse us from all un-righteousness.
Thanks be to God. (I John 1:9)

PSALTER   Psalm 116

SCRIPTURE *(a time of silence follows each reading)*
Exodus 12:1-14
1 Corinthians 11: 23-26
John 13: 1-15

CANTICLE OF REDEMPTION *(De Profundis,* see page 42)

COLLECT
O God whose Chosen One teaches true humility: Wash from us the stain of sin. Grant that, inspired by the example of Christ, we may serve all at every time in every place. In all times of trial may we offer Christ; to whom be praise and honor for ever and ever. **Amen.**
[GLH]

[FOOTWASHING:
(During the footwashing, UMH 432 *and* 549 *may be sung)*

[EUCHARIST *(if not observed in another service on this day)*
[See "The Great Thanksgiving for Holy Thursday Evening, pages 64-65, *UMBOW*]

COLLECT
O Lover of souls, whose mercy is declared again and again in the Meal you instituted: so compose our hearts in yielding up this day to you that our spirits realize we have been reconciled to you, that awaking to the morning's light we will know ourselves to be bound anew in holy covenant with you in your cross and passion for the world. **Amen.** [DTB]

[THE LORD'S PRAYER *(if not prayed during Eucharist)*

[STRIPPING OF THE CHURCH *(in silence)*

GOING FORTH IN SILENCE
[Note: This office, along with others which follow, is not completed until the Great Paschal Vigil. As a sign that we await the coming celebration of the resurrection, these offices do not conclude in the usual way.]

COMPLINE FOR HOLY THURSDAY

CALL TO PRAYER
Let us be going out to the Mount of Olives with Christ.
We will not desert you, O Lord.

NIGHT HYMN "Go to Dark Gethsemane" (*UMH* 290 st. 1-2)

PRAYER OF CONFESSION
O good Shepherd, who laid down your life for the sheep, remember us:
Lord, not our will, but yours be done.
O everlasting Power and Wisdom of the most high God, Word of God, remember us:
Lord, not our will, but yours be done.
O Maker of the world, the Life of all, the Lord of angels, remember us:
Lord, not our will, but yours be done.
O Lamb of God, who for us was led as a sheep to the slaughter, remember us:
Lord, not our will, but yours be done.
O You who were seized, though guiltless, were buffeted, and given over to robbers, remember us:
Lord, not our will, but yours be done.
You who alone by your death have overcome the death of our guilt, remember us:
Lord, not our will, but yours be done.

[ADAPTED FROM MOZARABIC BREVIARY; TAR]

The saying is sure and worthy of full acceptance, that Christ Jesus came into the world to save sinners. If any one sins, we have an advocate with God, Jesus Christ the righteous; and he is the atoning sacrifice for our sins, and not for ours only but also for the sins of the whole world.
Thanks be to God. (1 JOHN 2:1B-2)

PSALTER
Our help is in the name of the Lord;
who made heaven and earth.

Psalm 80

Glory to you, most blessed and holy Trinity,
One God, now and forever. Amen..

SCRIPTURE
       Year A: Mt. 26: 30-46
       Year B: Mk. 14: 26-42
       Year C: Lk. 22: 39-46

--silence--

PRAYERS
THE KYRIE   *(spoken)*
Lord, have mercy upon us.
Lord, have mercy upon us.
Lord, have mercy upon us.

Christ, have mercy upon us.
Christ, have mercy upon us.
Christ have mercy upon us.

Lord, have mercy upon us.
Lord, have mercy upon us.
Lord, have mercy upon us.

COLLECT

Good Lord, give me the grace, in all my fear and
agony, to have recourse to that great fear and agony
that you, my Savior, had at the Mount of Olives
before your most bitter passion, and as I meditate on
it, may I receive comfort, consolation, and strength
for my soul. **Amen.**   [ST. THOMAS MORE, 1474-1535]

THE LORD'S PRAYER

COMMENDATION

Guide us waking, O Lord, and guard us sleeping,
that awake we may watch with Christ,
and asleep we may rest in peace.
May the divine help remain with us always.
And with those who are absent from us.

--silence--

Into your hands, O Lord, I commend my spirit,
For you have redeemed me, O Lord,
O God of Truth.

[ADAPTED FROM PS. 4:8, THE SARUM BREVIARY, AND PS. 30:5, TJC]

--Let all depart in silence--

VIGIL FOR HOLY THURSDAY

THE SERVICE OF LIGHT *(a candle is lit in silence)*

THANKSGIVING FOR THE LIGHT

On this, the night of your betrayal O Lord, your light
flickered dimly in the garden. Although you were
apprehended, we, your disciples, cannot comprehend
the love with which your prayers were offered. Your
light, O Lord shines in the darkness of this world, yet
we fear the overwhelming cloak of darkness which

surrounds us this night. Illumine us, O Lord, that when those who are jealous of its splendor seek to conceal your light, you may shine ever more brightly through us. We pray to you, O God of light, through Jesus Christ our Lord. **Amen..**

[TAR]

--silence--

(the candle may be hidden under a container which will allow it to breathe and to be seen only dimly, symbolizing Christ's captivity)

THE SERVICE OF THE WORD

PRAYER FOR ILLUMINATION
O Lord, we wait and watch with great anxiety and anticipation. Fill us with the light of your Spirit that we may hear again the story of our salvation. **Amen.**

[TAR]

THE LESSONS
(After the reading of each of the seven lessons, a time of silence is observed. The length of the silence should be determined by the desired length of the   service.)

Isaiah 53:1-4

Psalm 130 (alternate reading: Psalm 131)

1 Peter 2: 19-23

Year A:	Year B:	Year C:
Mt. 26:47-56	Mk. 14:43-52	Lk.22:47-53
Mt. 26:57-68	Mk. 14:53-65	Lk. 22:63-71
Mt. 27:1-2, 11-14	Mk. 15:1-5	Lk. 23:1-5,13-16
Mt. 27:15-26	Mk. 15:6-15	Lk. 23:18-25

CANTICLE OF LIGHT AND DARKNESS (*UMH* 205; Response 2)

116

PRAYER
Today, O good Jesus, for our sakes you did not hide your
face from shame and spitting.
Today, Jesus our Redeemer, for us you were mocked,
struck by unbelievers and crowned with thorns.
Today, O good Jesus, you laid down your life on the
cross for the sheep, and were crucified with robbers, and
had nails driven through your hands and feet.
Today, O good Jesus, put an end to our sins that on the
day of resurrection we may be raised up to everlasting
life. **Amen.**   [MOZARABIC SACRAMENTARY; ALT. TJC]

--silence--

CONCLUDING COLLECT
Be with us, merciful God, and protect us through the
silent hours of this night, so that we, who are wearied by
the changes and chances of this fleeting world, may rest
upon your eternal changelessness; through Jesus Christ
our Lord. **Amen.**   [BCP]

--Depart in silence--

MORNING PRAYER FOR
GOOD FRIDAY

CALL TO PRAYER
Lord, we are ready to go with you to prison and
death!
but you know that we will yet deny you.

[HYMN "O Sacred Head, Now Wounded" (*UMH* 286) or
"To Mock Your Reign, O Dearest Lord" (*UMH* 285)

INVITATION

Let us exalt our minds, kindle our hearts; let us not quench our spirits, but let us lay aside tiresome arguments and attach ourselves to the one on the cross. If it seems right, let us all go along with Peter to the house of Caiaphas, and with him, let us cry to Christ the words of Peter long ago-- "Even if he goes to the cross and enters the tomb-- We suffer with you, and we shall die with you and cry: 'Hasten, Holy One, save your sheep.'"
Amen.   [ROMANOS, 6TH C.]

PSALTER   Psalm 40: 1-11

SCRIPTURE
Year A: Mt. 26: 69-75
Year B: Mk. 14: 66-72
Year C: Lk. 22: 54-62

--silence--

CANTICLE OF ZECHARIAH (*Benedictus*, spoken; see page 20)

PRAYERS OF INTERCESSION AND SUPPLICATION

O most great and mighty God, enable us to do everything which you have commanded us, heartily, with good will and true love to your service.

Render us so mindful of the great love of our Lord that we may be zealously concerned for his glory and use our utmost diligence to commemorate his death and passion, making a joyful sacrifice of our souls and bodies to him, and earnestly desiring that his kingdom may come over all the earth.

Fulfill, most merciful Lord, all our petitions:
Especially, we pray for those who suffer ...
for those who struggle to remain faithful ...

for those who seek the courage of their convictions ...
for those who walk a lonely road ...
for your church, its ministry and mission...
for our suffering world ...

Help us not to deny you, O Lord Jesus, but to proclaim
your name for ever. **Amen.** [ADAPTED FROM JOHN WESLEY; TAR]

THE LORD'S PRAYER

[HYMN "O Love Divine, What Hast Thou Done" (*UMH* 287)

CONCLUDING PRAYER
O Lord, do not withhold your mercy;
let your steadfast love preserve me. (PSALM 40: 11)

--Depart in silence--

MID-MORNING PRAYER FOR GOOD FRIDAY

OPENING SENTENCES
God forbid that I should glory, save in the Cross of
our Lord Jesus Christ.
**God be merciful to us, and bless us, and shine
your divine countenance upon us.** [ADAPTED; WPM]

PRAYER
Lord, by shedding his blood for us, your Son, Jesus
Christ, established the paschal mystery. In your good-
ness, make us holy and watch over us always. **Amen.**
[ROMAN RITE]

PSALTER
Psalm 95: 6-11

THE "LITTLE CHAPTER"

In the days when he was in the flesh, Christ offered prayers and supplications with loud cries and tears to God, who was able to save him from death, and he was heard because of his reverence. Son though he was, he learned obedience through what he suffered; and having been made perfect, he became the source of eternal salvation for all who obey him. (Hebrews 5: 7-9)

--silence--

COLLECT

Almighty God, whose most dear Son went not up to joy but first he suffered pain, and entered not into glory before he was crucified; Mercifully grant that we, walking in the way of the cross, may find it none other than the way of life and peace; through the same your Son Jesus Christ our Lord. **Amen.** [American Prayer Book]

THE LORD'S PRAYER

--Depart in silence--

PRAYERS OF THE HOURS
OF THE CRUCIFIXION

(prayed between noon and three on Good Friday)

GATHERING *in silence*

GREETING

Christ himself bore our sins in his body on the tree.
That we might die to sin and live to righteousness.
Blessed be the name of the Lord our God
who redeems us from sin and death.

COLLECT

Almighty God, graciously behold this your family, for whom our Lord Jesus Christ was willing to be betrayed and given into the hands of sinners, and to be lifted high upon the cross so that he might draw the whole world to himself. Grant that we, who glory in his death for our salvation, may also glory in his call to take up our cross and follow him; through the same Jesus Christ our Lord. **Amen.** [TRADITIONAL GOOD FRIDAY COLLECTS ALT]

HYMN "Sing My Tongue the Glorious Battle" (*UMH* 296)

LITANY OF CONFESSION AND PETITION

[In place of the spoken response, the Kyrie *may be said or sung. See* UMH *483)*

O Jesus, who did cleanse the lepers, heal the sick, and give sight to the blind, heal the diseases of our souls, open our eyes and fix them on our high calling, and cleanse our hearts from every desire which hinders the advancing of your glory.
Hear our prayer, O Lord.
O Jesus, poor and abject, unknown and despised, have mercy on us and let us not be ashamed to follow you.
Hear our prayer, O Lord.
O Jesus, hated, calumniated, and persecuted, have mercy upon us and let us not be afraid to come after you.
Hear our prayer, O Lord.
O Jesus, blasphemed, accused, and wrongfully condemned, have mercy upon us and teach us to endure the contradiction of sinners.
Hear our prayer, O Lord.
O Jesus, clothed with a habit of reproach and shame, have mercy upon us and let us not seek our own glory.
Hear our prayer, O Lord.
O Jesus, insulted, mocked, and spit upon, have mercy upon us and let us run with patience the race set before us.
Hear our prayer, O Lord.

O Jesus, dragged to the pillar, scourged, and bathed in blood, have mercy upon us and let us not faint in the fiery trial.

Hear our prayer, O Lord.

O Jesus, crowned with thorns and hailed in derision;

Have mercy on us.

O Jesus, burdened with our sins and the curses of the people;

Have mercy on us.

O Jesus, affronted, outraged, buffeted, overwhelmed with injuries, griefs, and humiliations;

Have mercy on us.

O Jesus, hanging on the accursed tree, bowing the head, giving up the ghost, have mercy upon us and conform our souls and bodies to your holy, humble, suffering Spirit.

Hear our prayer, O Lord. Amen.

[ADAPTED FROM JOHN WESLEY, *PERSONAL PRAYERS*, TAR]

OLD TESTMENT LESSON   Isaiah 52:13-53:12

PSALTER   Psalm 22

EPISTLE LESSON   Hebrews 10:16-25

RESPONSORY

Christ became obedient unto death, even death on a cross.

Have mercy on us, Lord Jesus.

WORDS FROM THE CROSS

Luke 23:32-38

"Father, forgive them; for they do not know what they are doing."

--silence--

Christ, who forgave those who crucified you: teach us to forgive those who wrong us. Give us grace to confess our sin. May we receive your forgiveness with thankful hearts. Hear us, Holy Jesus. Amen.   [DWV]

122

[HYMN "Jesus, Keep Me Near the Cross" (*UMH* 301)

Luke 23:39-43
"Truly I tell you, today you will be with me in Paradise."

--silence--

Lord Jesus Christ, whose word to the thief fills us with hope: teach us to trust in you in life and death. Give us grace to receive your gift of eternal life so that even in suffering we may share your love. Hear us, Holy Jesus. Amen. [DWV]

[RESPONSE "Jesus, Remember Me" (*UMH* 488)

John 19:23-27
"Woman, here is your son." "Here is your mother."

--silence--

Lord Jesus Christ, who spoke words of care from the cross, teach us how to love those for whom we care. Release us from slavery to self so that we may enable others to be free. Give us all grace to serve you as we serve each other. Hear us, Holy Jesus. Amen. [DWV]

[HYMN "Beneath the Cross of Jesus" (UMH # 297)

Mark 15:33-36
"My God, my God, why have you forsaken me?"

--silence--

Lord Jesus Christ, who knows our hours of anguish, teach us to be honest about our feelings. Give us grace to call out to you when we feel abandoned, with the assurance that your love never fails. Hear us, Holy Jesus. Amen. [DWV]

[HYMN "O Sacred Head Now Wounded" (*UMH* 287)

Matthew 27:39-43; John 19:28-29
"I am thirsty."

--silence--

Lord Jesus Christ, you cry to us that you are thirsty, yet we have nothing that will satisfy. Even though we have nothing of our own to offer, fill us with your living water that we may offer it to others in your name. Give us grace to yearn for a world in which the hungry are fed and the oppressed set free. Hear us, Holy Jesus. Amen. [TAR;DWV]

[HYMN "O Crucified Redeemer" (*UMH* 425)

Luke 23:44-46a
"Father, into your hands I commend my spirit."

--silence--

Lord Jesus Christ, who trusted in God in the face of death: teach us how to live and die as persons of faith. Give us grace to place ourselves in the hands of God, knowing that there is nothing in all creation which can separate us from your love. Hear us, Holy Jesus. Amen. [DWV]

[HYMN "O Love Divine, What Hast Thou Done" (*UMH* 287)

--silence--

[The *Kyrie* is sung (see *UMH* 483). This is the last time music is used in the triduum until the Great Paschal Vigil of Easter.]

John 19:30-37
"It is finished."

--silence--

Lord Jesus Christ, who came to set us free: let the shadow of your cross fall upon us in this hour that we may wonder at the gift of your redeeming love, and be empowered by your Spirit to take up our own cross daily and follow you. Amen. [BB]

MEDITATION AT THE CROSS

SILENT MEDITATION

THE REPROACHES:
CHRIST'S LAMENT AGAINST HIS FAITHLESS CHURCH

O my people, O my Church, what have I done to you, or in what have I offended you? I led you forth from the land of Egypt and delivered you by the waters of baptism, but you have prepared a cross for your Savior.

> R   **Holy God, holy and mighty,**
> **holy and immortal One, have mercy upon us.**

--silence--

I led you through the desert forty years and fed you with manna; I brought you through times of persecution and of renewal and gave you my body, the bread of heaven; but you have prepared a cross for your Savior.   **R**

--silence--

I made you branches of my vineyard and gave you the water of salvation, but when I was thirsty you gave me vinegar and gall and pierced with a spear the side of your Savior.   **R**

--silence--

I went before you in a pillar of cloud, but you have led me to the judgment hall of Pilate. I brought you to a land of freedom and prosperity, but you have scourged, mocked, and beaten me.   **R**

--silence--

I gave you a royal scepter, and bestowed the keys to the kingdom, but you have given me a crown of thorns. I raised you on high with great power, but you have hanged me on the cross. **R**

--silence--

My peace I gave, which the world cannot give, and washed your feet as a servant, but you draw the sword to strike in my name and seek high places in my kingdom. **R**

--silence--

I accepted the cup of suffering and death for your sakes, but you scatter and deny and abandon me. I sent the Spirit of truth to lead you, but you close your hearts to guidance. **R**

--silence--

I called you to go and bring forth fruit, but you cast lots for my clothing. I prayed that you all may be one, but you continue to quarrel and divide. **R**

--silence--

I grafted you into the tree of my chosen people Israel, but you turned on them with persecution and mass murder. I made you joint heirs with them of my covenants, but you made them scapegoats for your own guilt. **R**

-silence-

I came to you as the least of your brothers and sisters. I was hungry but you gave me no food, thirsty but you gave me no drink. I was a stranger but you did not welcome me, naked but you did not clothe me, sick and in prison but you did not visit me. **R**

SILENT MEDITATION

THE LORD'S PRAYER

--Depart in silence--

EVENING PRAYER FOR GOOD FRIDAY

OPENING SENTENCES
O God, come to our assistance.
O Lord, hasten to help us.

PRAYER
Merciful God: As Jesus suffered the shame of the cross for us, grant that we may be willing to pay any price for the salvation of others. Save us from hardness of heart! Help us receive the One who died for us so that we may repent, confess our sins, and be inspired to share your overflowing love; through Jesus Christ your Sacrifice. **Amen.** [GLH]

PSALTER Psalm 69: 1-18

SCRIPTURE
Year A: Mt. 27: 57-61
Year B: Mk. 15: 42-47
Year C: Lk. 23: 50-56

--silence--

LITANY
Joseph went to Pilate, pleaded with him and cried out:
Give me that Stranger
  Who since his youth
  Has wandered as a stranger.
Give me that Stranger
  Upon whom I look with wonder,
  Seeing him a guest of death.
Give me that Stranger
  Whom envious ones
  Estrange from the world.
Give me that Stranger
  That I may bury him in a tomb,

Who being a stranger has no place
Whereupon to lay his head.
Give me that Stranger
To whom his mother cried out
As she saw him dead:
"My Son, my senses are wounded
And my heart is burned
As I see you dead!
Yet, trusting in your resurrection,
I magnify you!"
In such words did the honorable Joseph plead with
Pilate. He took the Savior's body and, with fear, wrapped
it in linen with spices. And he placed you in a tomb
O you who grant everlasting life and great mercy to
us all. [ORTHODOX LITURGY]

--silence--

CANTICLE OF REDEMPTION   (*UMH* 516)

PRAYERS OF INTERCESSION AND SUPPLICATION

Almighty God, you sent your Son into the world, not to
condemn the world, but that the world through him
might be saved; that all who believe in him might be
delivered from the power of sin and death, and become
heirs with him of everlasting life. We pray, therefore, for
people everywhere according to their needs.

Let us pray for the holy catholic church of Christ throughout the world that God will confirm the church in faith,
increase it in love and preserve it in peace.

--silence--

Let us pray for all nations and peoples of the earth, and
for those in authority among them that by God's help
they may seek justice and truth, and live in peace and
concord.

--silence--

Let us pray for all who suffer and are afflicted in body or in mind that God in mercy will comfort and relieve them, and grant them the knowledge of God's love, and stir up in us the will and patience to minister to their needs.

--silence--

Let us pray for all who have not received the Gospel of Christ that God will open their hearts to the truth, and lead them to faith and obedience.

--silence--

O God, who for our redemption gave your only be-gotten Son to the death of the Cross, and has delivered us from the power of the enemy, grant us to die daily to sin, that we may evermore live with you, through the same Jesus Christ our Lord. **Amen.**

[ADAPTED FROM GREGORY THE GREAT AND BCP; TAR]

THE LORD'S PRAYER

--Depart in silence--

VIGIL

[This office replaces both Compline and Mid-Night Matins; It may be prayed as an office, or used as the basis of an all-night vigil.]

OPENING SENTENCES

O God, come to our assistance.
O Lord hasten to help us.

COLLECT

Lord Jesus Christ, who this night rested in the tomb and so sanctified the grave to be a bed of hope to your people: make us deeply sorry for our sins so that when our days are earth are accomplished, we may live eternally with you; for with the Eternal Source of All and the Holy Spirit you live and reign, now and for ever. **Amen.**   [ANON]

SCRIPTURE   Isaiah 53:5-12

--silence--

RESPONSORY   Lamentations 1:1-2; 2:18-19
How lonely she is now, the once crowded city!
Widowed is she who was mistress over nations;
The princess among the provinces has been made a
toiling slave.
Bitterly she weeps at night, tears upon her cheeks,
With not one to console her of all her dear ones;
**Her friends have all betrayed her and become her
enemies.**
Cry aloud to the Lord O wall of daughter Zion!
Let tears stream down like a torrent day and night!
Give yourself no rest,
your eyes no respite!
Arise, cry out in the night, at the beginning of the
watches!
**Pour out your heart like water before the presence of
the Lord!**
Lift your hands to him for the lives of your children,
who faint for hunger at the head of every street.

PSALTER
*[In a longer vigil, all of the following psalms are used. In a
shorter vigil, at least one should be selected.]*

Ps. 2, 37 (1-11), 39, 43, 80

EPISTLE Hebrews 10:19-25

GOSPEL LESSON
Year A: Mt. 24:36-44
Year B: Mk. 13:32-37
Year C: Lk. 21:34-46

--silence--

LITANY OF PETITION

Soul of Christ,
    be my sanctification;
Body of Christ,
    be my salvation;
Blood of Christ,
    fill all my veins;
Water of Christ's side,
    wash out my stains;
Passion of Christ,
    my comfort be;
O good Jesus,
    listen to me:
In your wounds I fain would hide,
    Ne'er to be parted from your side;
Guard me, should the foes assail me;
    Call me when my life shall fail me,
Bid me come to you above,
    With your saints to sing your love,
    world without end. Amen..

[ANIMA CHRISTI, 14TH C. TR. JOHN HENRY NEWMAN, 1801-90]

THE *KYRIE* *(spoken)*

Lord, have mercy upon us.
    Christ have mercy upon us.
Lord, have mercy upon us.

COMMENDATION

In peace we will lie down and sleep.
    In the Lord alone we safely rest.
Guide us waking, O Lord, and guard us sleeping,
    that awake we may watch with Christ,
    and asleep we may rest in peace.
May the divine help remain with us always.
    And with those who are absent from us.

--silence--

Into your hands, O Lord, I commend my spirit,
For you have redeemed me, O Lord, O God of Truth.

CANTICLE OF SIMEON (*Nunc Dimittis*, spoken only)
Lord, you have now set your servant free
to go in peace as you have promised;
for these eyes of mine have seen the Savior,
Whom you have prepared for all the world to see.
A Light to enlighten the nations,
And the glory of your people Israel.

--silence--

COLLECT
O Lord, my God, we sing to you a burial song and a
funeral chant, who by your entombment has opened for
us a door to life, and by your dying has brought an end
to our death and hell. In sleep we lie down with you to
rise to morning's light. Grant us a peaceful rest and a
perfect end. **Amen.**

[ADAPTED FROM HOLY SATURDAY ORTHODOX LITURGY; DTB]

THE LORD'S PRAYER

--Depart in silence--

MORNING PRAYER FOR HOLY SATURDAY
(The Great Sabbath)

OPENING SENTENCES
Out of the depths I cry to you, O LORD.
Lord, hear my voice!
Come, faithful, come, let us keep watch beside
Christ's tomb,
**He who gives life to those who live among the
tombs.**

Come, let us cry out with the voice of the psalmist:
What profit is there in death?
Will the dust praise you?
Will it tell of your faithfulness?
Weeping may tarry for the night, but joy comes in the morning.
"Arise, O Lord! Let not mortals prevail,
Lift up your hand; forget not the afflicted."

[ADAPTED FROM HOLY SATURDAY ORTHODOX LITURGY; TAR]
(Ps. 30:9; 9:19, 10:12)

MORNING COLLECT

Almighty and everlasting God, the comfort of the sad, the strength of sufferers, let the prayers of those that cry out of any tribulation come unto you, that all may rejoice to find that your mercy is present with them in their afflictions; through Jesus Christ our Lord. **Amen.**

[GELASIAN SACRAMENTARY, 5TH C.]

PSALTER   Psalm 130

SCRIPTURE Matthew 27: 62-66

CANTICLE OF ZECHARIAH (*Benedictus*, see p. 20, spoken only)

PRAYERS OF INTERCESSION AND SUPPLICATION

Creator and Architect of earth and all stars, cause us to rest from our labors on this holy sabbath as you rested from your work. Cause us to anticipate the rest that comes in death as we remember Jesus in the tomb; the rest that comes to those who are spent, exhausted, inert. Cause us to wait in hope for the break of day and the resurrection.

Remember those who have died and those who mourn their death...

Remember those who died through violence and the miscarriage of justice...

Remember those who died confessing your name for the sake of the Gospel...

133

Remember those who resist trusting you in life and
in death...
Remember those who cannot rest...
And remember us in our restless thoughts,
strivings, and failures... [DTB]

COLLECT
O ruler of the ages, through your passion, you fulfilled
the plan of salvation. As you keep Sabbath in the tomb,
you grant us a new Sabbath. Unto you we cry aloud:
Arise, O Lord, judge the earth, for measureless is your
great mercy, reigning for ever. **Amen.**

[ADAPTED FROM ORTHODOX HOLY SATURDAY MATINS; TAR]

THE LORD'S PRAYER

--Depart in silence--

MID-MORNING PRAYER FOR HOLY SATURDAY

OPENING SENTENCES
Out of the depths I cry to you, O LORD.
Lord, hear my voice!

PRAYER
Jesus my Lord,
Come to me,
Comfort me, console me.
Visit the hearts
In strange lands
Yearning for you.
Visit the dying and those
Who have died without you.
Jesus, my Lord,
Visit also those
Who persecute you.

134

Lord Jesus, you are my light
In the darkness.
You are my warmth
In the cold.
You are my happiness
In sorrow...   [ANONYMOUS]

PSALTER   Psalm 42:1-6a

SCRIPTURE   Job 14:1-14

--silence--

RESPONSORY
Let the same mind be in you that was in Christ Jesus,
who, though he was in the form of God,
did not regard equality with God
as something to be exploited,
but emptied himself,
taking the form of a slave,
being born in human likeness.
And being found in human form,
he humbled himself
and became obedient to the point of death--
even death on a cross.   (PHILIPPIANS 2: 5-8)

[SILENT PRAYER

COLLECT
Gracious God, keep us this day in your fear and favor,
and teach us in all our thoughts, words, and works to
live to your glory. If you guide us not, we go astray; if
you uphold us not, we fall. Let your good providence
be our defense and your good Spirit our guide and
counselor, and supporter in all our ways. And grant that
we may do always what is acceptable in your sight,
through Jesus Christ our Lord, in whose holy name we
lift up these our imperfect prayers:
Our Father...
                                    [JOHN WESLEY, FROM PRAYERS OF JW]

--Depart in silence--

135

MID-DAY PRAYER FOR HOLY SATURDAY

OPENING SENTENCES
Out of the depths I cry to you, O LORD.
Lord, hear my voice!

PRAYER
O God, by the suffering of Christ your Son you have saved us from death. We bear the likeness of sinful humanity. May the sanctifying power of grace help us to put on the likeness of Jesus Christ. In your goodness raise up your faithful people buried with him in baptism, to be one with him in your love. **Amen.**

[ADAPTED ROMAN RITE & ROMAN LITURGY OF THE HOURS; TAR;DWV)

PSALTER: Psalm 42: 6b-11

THE *KYRIE* (spoken)
Lord, have mercy.
Lord, have mercy.
Lord, have mercy.

Christ, have mercy.
Christ, have mercy.
Christ, have mercy.

Lord, have mercy.
Lord, have mercy.
Lord, have mercy.

SCRIPTURE   Jeremiah 20: 7-12

--silence--

RESPONSORY
We know that the whole creation has been groaning in labor pains until now;

136

and not only the creation, but we ourselves, who have the first fruits of the Spirit, groan inwardly while we wait for adoption, the redemption of our bodies.

For in hope we were saved.

Now hope that is seen is not hope. For who hopes for what is seen? But if we hope for what we do not see, we wait for it with patience. (Romans 8:22-25)

[SILENT PRAYER

COLLECT

O Lord, who washes out all our offenses, comfort us who faithfully call upon you; blot out our transgressions, and restore us from death to the land of the living; through Christ our Lord. **Amen.**

[Sarum Breviary, 11th c.]

THE LORD'S PRAYER (spoken)

--Depart in silence--

MID-AFTERNOON PRAYER FOR HOLY SATURDAY

OPENING SENTENCES

Out of the depths I cry to you, O LORD.

Lord, hear my voice!

PRAYER

O Merciful God, who answers the poor,

Answer us.

O Merciful God, who answers the lowly in spirit,

Answer us.

O Merciful God, who answers the broken of heart,

Answer us.

O Merciful God,
   Answer us.
O Merciful God,
   Have compassion.
O Merciful God,
   Redeem.
O Merciful God,
   Save.
O Merciful God, have pity upon us,
   Now,
   Speedily,
   And at a near time. Amen..

[JEWISH PRAYER ON DAY OF ATONEMENT]

PSALTER   Psalm 31: 9-16

SCRIPTURE   Isaiah 51:9-11

--silence--

RESPONSORY
   Set your minds on things that are above, not on things
   that are on earth, for you have died, and your life is
   hidden with Christ in God.
   When Christ who is your life is revealed, then
   you also will be revealed with him in glory.

(COLOSSIANS 3: 2-4)

[SILENT PRAYER

COLLECT
   Most merciful God, the helper of all, so strengthen us by
   your power that our sorrow may be turned into joy, and
   we may continually glorify your holy name; through
   Jesus Christ our Lord. **Amen.**   [SARUM BREVIARY, 11TH C.]

THE LORD'S PRAYER (spoken)

--Depart in silence--

EVENING PRAYER FOR HOLY SATURDAY

OPENING SENTENCES
> Out of the depths I cry to you, O LORD.
> **Lord, hear my voice!**

PRAYER OF CONFESSION AND PARDON
> Our God and God of our ancestors, let our prayer reach you do not turn away from our pleading. We are not so arrogant and obstinate to claim that we are indeed righteous people and have never sinned. But we know that both we and our ancestors have sinned.
> We have abused and betrayed. We are cruel.
> We have destroyed and embittered other people's lives.
> We are false to ourselves.
> We have gossiped about others and hated them.
> We have insulted and jeered. We have killed. We have lied.
> We have misled others and neglected them.
> We were obstinate. We have perverted and quarelled.
> We have robbed and stolen.
> We have transgressed through unkindness.
> We have been both violent and weak.
> We have practiced extortion.
> We have yielded to wrong desires, our zeal was misplaced.
>
> We turn away from your commandments and good judgement but it does not help us. your justice exists whatever happens to us, for you work for truth, but we bring about evil. What can we say before you so distant is the place where you are found? And what can we tell you? Your being is remote as the heavens? Yet you know everything, hidden and revealed. You know the mys-

teries of the universe and the intimate secrets of everyone alive. You probe our body's state. You see into the
heart and mind. Nothing escapes you, nothing is hidden from your gaze.

Our God and God of our ancestors, have mercy on us
and pardon all our sins; grant atonement for all our
iniquities, forgiveness for all our transgressions.

[JEWISH CONFESSION FOR DAY OF ATONEMENT]

--silence--

For God so loved the world that God's only begotten Son
was given that whoever believes in him should not
perish but have eternal life. (JOHN 3:16 ALT)

PSALTER   Psalm 31: 1-5

SCRIPTURE   1 Peter 4: 1-8

--silence--

CANTICLE OF HOPE (spoken only) [see *UMH* 734]

--silent prayer--

THE LORD'S PRAYER (spoken)

DEPARTURE
The time that the Israelites had lived in Egypt was four
hundred thirty years. At the end of four hundred thirty
years, on that very day, all the companies of the LORD
went out from the land of Egypt. That was for the LORD
a night of vigil, to bring them up out of the land of Egypt.
**That same night is a vigil to be kept for the
LORD throughout all generations.**

(ADAPTED FROM EXODUS 12: 40-42)

Therefore, let us go forth, keeping vigil for the Lord.

--Depart in silence--

THE GREAT PASCHAL VIGIL:

The First Service of Easter

(This, the most holy and joyful festival of the Christian year, celebrates the whole story of salvation history culminating in the paschal mystery of Christ's death and resurrection. Through Light, Word, Water, and Feast we experience anew our pass-over from bondage to freedom, from death to life. This service should be a "people's office" open to the whole congregation. Only when circumstances make that impossible or unwise should this office be prayed apart from the congregation. Even then, it is prayed in concert with Christians of all times and places, whether dispersed or gathered.)

THE SERVICE OF LIGHT

GATHERING (in silence as a new fire is kindled)

GREETING AND INTRODUCTION

Dear friends in Christ, on this most holy night, when our Lord Jesus Christ passed from death to life, we gather as the Church to watch and pray. We will celebrate Christ's baptism and his holy resurrection which gives us life and salvation. This is thepassover of Christ, in which, by hearing his Word and celebrating his Sacraments, we share in his victory over death.

[ADAPT FROM BCP & 4TH C. PRAYER; TAR]

OPENING PRAYER

O Savior Jesus Christ, grant light to our minds and hearts. Enlighten us as you enlightened the women who came to your tomb with spices, so they could anoint your body, the source of life. Since you have raised us up and delivered us from the darkness of sin and death, give us grace through your loving kindness that we may kindle our lamps with the light of your radiant and glorious resurrection. **Amen.**

[ADAPTED FROM ORTHODOX LITURGY; TAR; DWV]

LIGHTING OF THE PASCHAL CANDLE

Hear the Word of God:

In the beginning was the Word and the Word was with God and the Word was God. ... In him was life, and the life was the light of all. The light shines in the darkness and the darkness has not overcome it. (JOHN 1:1, 4-5)

PROCESSION

(if there is a congregational candlelight procession, the following invitation may be issued:)

Come, O Faithful, and take light from the Light that never fades; come and glorify Christ who is risen from the dead!

Christ is risen from the dead!
He has crushed death by his death
and bestowed life upon those who lay in the tomb.

[ORTHODOX LITURGY]

(During the procession the leader pauses three times and the following litany is sung)

EXSULTET

(The Exsultet *may be spoken, chanted, or sung to an improvised melody.)*

Rejoice, heavenly powers! Sing, choirs of angels!
Exult, all creation 'round God's throne!
Jesus Christ, our King, is risen!
Sound the trumpet of salvation! **R**

Rejoice, O earth, in shining splendor,
   radiant in the brightness of our King!
Christ has conquered! Glory fills you!
Darkness vanishes for ever! **R**

Rejoice, O holy Church! Exult in glory!
The risen Savior shines upon you!
Let this place resound with joy,
   echoing the mighty song of all God's people! **R**

It is truly right that we should praise you,
invisible, almighty, and eternal God,
   and your Son, Jesus Christ.
For Christ has ransomed us with his blood,
and paid the debt of Adam's sin
to deliver your faithful people! **R**

This is our Passover feast,
   when Christ, the true Lamb, is slain.
This is the night when first you saved our forbears.
You freed the people of Israel from their slavery
and led them with dry feet through the sea. **R**

This is the night when the pillar of fire destroyed the
darkness of sin!
This is the night when Christians everywhere,
   washed clean of sin and freed from all defilement,
   are restored to grace and grow together in holiness.
This is the night when Jesus Christ broke the chains
   of death and rose triumphant from the grave.
Night truly blessed, when heaven is wedded to earth,
   and we are reconciled to you! **R**

143

Accept this Easter candle, a flame divided <u>but</u>
   undimmed,
   a pillar of fire that glows <u>to</u> your honor.
Let it mingle with the <u>lights</u> of heaven,
   and continue bravely burning
   to dispel the darkness <u>of</u> the night! **R**

May the Morning Star, which never sets,
   find this <u>flame</u> still burning.
Christ, that Morning Star, who came back <u>from</u> the dead,
who shed his peaceful light on <u>all</u> creation,
   your Son who lives and reigns for <u>ever</u> and ever. **R**
                                                    [UMBOW]

THE SERVICE OF THE WORD

INTRODUCTION
   Let us hear the record of God's saving deeds and pray
   that our God will bring each of us to the fullness of
   redemption.   [BCP]

THE CREATION
   Genesis 1:1-2:4a

                    --silence--

   [Psalm 33

   O God, who wonderfully created, and yet more wonderfully restored, the dignity of human nature: Grant
   that we may share the divine life of him who humbled
   himself to share our humanity, your Son Jesus Christ our
   Lord. **Amen.**   [BCP]

   [HYMN "Morning Has Broken" (*UMH* 145)

THE FLOOD
   Genesis 7:1-5, 11-18; 8:6-18; 9:8-13

                    --silence--

   [Psalm 46
144

Almighty God of heaven and earth, you set in the clouds a rainbow to be a sign of your covenant with all living things: Grant that we, who are saved through water and the Spirit, may know again the mark of your covenant with us in baptism through Jesus Christ our Lord. **Amen.**   [BCP ALT TAR]

[HYMN "Faith, While Trees Are Still in Blossom"
   (*UMH* 508; stanzas 1-3 and 5)

ABRAHAM'S TRUST IN GOD
Genesis 22: 1-18
                              --silence--

[Psalm 16

Gracious God of all believers, through Abraham's trust in your promise you made known your faithful love to countless numbers. By the grace of Christ's sacrifice fulfill in your Church and in all creation the joy of your promise and new covenant. **Amen.**   [UMBOW]

[HYMN "The God of Abraham Praise" (*UMH* 116, stanza 1)

ISRAEL'S DELIVERANCE AT THE RED SEA
Exodus 14:10-31
                              --silence--

[Canticle of Moses and Miriam   (*UMH* 135)

Lord God, in the new covenant you shed light on the miracles you worked in ancient times: the Red Sea is a symbol of our baptism, and the nation you freed from slavery is a sign of your Christian people. May every nation share the faith and privilege of Israel and come to new birth in the Holy Spirit. **Amen.**   [ROMAN RITE]

[HYMN "Come Ye Faithful, Raise the Strain"
   (*UMH* 315, stanza 1)

SALVATION OFFERED FREELY TO ALL
Isaiah 55: 1-5

--silence--

[Canticle of Covenant Faithfulness (*UMH* 125)

Creator of all things, you freely offer water to the thirsty and food to the hungry. Refresh us by the water of baptism and feed us with the bread and wine of your table, that your Word may bear fruit in our lives, and bring us all to your heavenly banquet; through Jesus Christ our Lord. **Amen.**   [UMBOW]

[HYMN "Guide Me, O Thou Great Jehovah" (*UMH* 127, stanza 1 & 2)

A NEW HEART AND A NEW SPIRIT
Ezekiel 36: 24-28

--silence--

[Psalm 51: 10-17

God of unchanging power and light, look with mercy and favor on your entire church. Bring lasting salvation to humankind, so that the world may see the fallen lifted up, the old made new, and all things brought to perfection, through him who is their origin, our Lord Jesus Christ. **Amen.**   [ROMAN RITE]

[RESPONSE "Spirit of the Living God" (*UMH* 393)

NEW LIFE FOR GOD'S PEOPLE
Ezekiel 37: 1-14

--silence--

[Psalm 143

Eternal God, you raised from the dead our Lord Jesus and by your Holy Spirit brought to life your Church. Breathe upon us again with your spirit and give new life to your people, through the same Jesus Christ our Redeemer. **Amen.**   [UMBOW]

146

[HYMN "Breathe On Me Breath of God" (*UMH* 420)

BURIED AND RAISED WITH CHRIST IN BAPTISM
Romans 6: 3-11

--silence--

Psalm 114

Let us chant Alleluia. Then the word of scripture will be accomplished, the word not of combatants any more, but of victors;
   Death has been swallowed up in victory.
Let us chant Alleluia.
   O Death, where is your sting?
Let us chant Alleluia.
        The sting of death is sin,
   you will seek its place and will not find it.
Let us chant Alleluia here in the midst of dangers and temptations, we and the others.
   God is faithful and will not allow us to be
   tempted above our ability.

O Blessed Alleluia of heaven! No more anguish, no more adversity. No more enemy. No more love of destruction. Up above, praise to God, and here below, praise to God. Praise mingled with fear here, but without disturbance above. here the one who chants must die, but there will we live for ever. here we chant in hope, there, in possession; here it is Alleluia on the way; route, there it is Alleluia on arriving home.

[AUGUSTINE, 5TH C.]

THE ALLELUIA*
(the first singing of the "Alleluia" in the daily office since Lent began)

(*UMH* 306; Antiphon only)

GOSPEL LESSON*   John 20: 1-18

147

HYMN* "The Day of Resurrection" (*UMH* 303)

RESPONSORY*
O death, where is your sting? O Grave, where is your victory? Christ is risen and you are abolished, Christ is risen and the demons are cast down, Christ is risen and the angels rejoice, Christ is risen and life is freed, Christ is risen and the tomb is emptied of the dead:
Christ, being risen from the dead, has become the Leader and Reviver of those who had fallen asleep. To him be glory and power for ever and ever. Amen!
[JOHN CHRYSOSTOM, 5TH C.]

[HOMILY

THE SERVICE OF WATER

HYMN "We Know That Christ Is Raised" (*UMH* 610)

INVITATION TO THE BAPTISMAL COVENANT
Brothers and sisters in Christ, we are bound together in the communion of all the saints by our baptism, through which we are initiated into Christ's holy church, dying and rising with Christ through God's grace. Therefore, let us come with faith in the company of the whole body of Christ.

LITANY OF THE SAINTS

Mary, blessed mother of our Lord,
R: Stand beside us.
Peter and Andrew, James, and John, disciples of our Lord, **R**
Mary Magdalene, Matthew, Mark, Luke and John, proclaimers of good news, **R**
Polycarp, Agnes, and Justin, martyrs and confessors, **R**
Athanasius, Augustine, and Basil, theologians of the faith, **R**

Luther and Calvin, Zwingli and Hus, reformers of the church, **R**

Francis and Clare, Benedict and Scholastica, seekers of the holy life, **R**

The Wesleys: Susanna, John and Charles, witnesses of grace, **R**

Victims of lynching, known and unknown, brothers and sisters of Stephen the martyr, **R**

Unnamed faithful ones in all times and places, baptized through death and life, **R**

THE BAPTISMAL COVENANT *(see* UMH *pp. 33 or 50; beginning after the introduction)*

THE SERVICE OF THE TABLE: THE EASTER FEAST

HYMN "Christian People: Raise Your Song" *(UMH 636)*

TAKING THE BREAD AND CUP

THE GREAT THANKSGIVING (see *UMBOW*, p. 66)

THE LORD'S PRAYER

BREAKING THE BREAD

GIVING THE BREAD AND CUP

PRAYER AFTER COMMUNION
We give glory to you, Lord, who raised up your cross to span the jaws of death like a bridge by which souls might pass from the region of the dead to the land of the living. You are incontestably alive. Your murderers sowed your living body in the earth as farmers sow grain, but it sprang up and yielded an abundant harvest of all those raised from the dead.

[ADAPTED FROM A PRAYER OF EPHREM THE SYRIAN, 4TH C.; DTB]
To you be all praise and glory! Thanks be to God!!

DISMISSAL WITH BLESSING
Now may the God of peace who brought back from the
dead our Lord Jesus, the great shepherd of the sheep, by
the blood of the eternal covenant, make you complete in
everything good so that you may do his will, working
among us that which is pleasing in his sight, through
Jesus Christ, to whom be the glory forever and ever!
[HEBREWS 13:20-21]

HYMN
"Christ the Lord Is Risen Today" (*UMH* 302) or
"Come Ye Faithful, Raise the Strain" (*UMH* 315; st. 2-5)

MORNING PRAYER FOR THE FESTIVAL OF THE RESURRECTION

CALL TO PRAISE AND PRAYER
O faithful, come on this day of the glorious resurrection!
**Let us drink the wine of the new vineyard, of the
divine joy, of the kingdom of Christ!**
Let us praise Christ, our God for ever and ever.
Alleluia!   [ORTHODOX LITURGY ALT; TAR]

HYMN   [77.77 with alleluias; Tune: *LLANFAIR, UMH* 312]
Jesus Christ is risen to day, Alleluia!
Our triumphant holy day, Alleluia!
Who did once upon the Cross, Alleluia!
Suffer to redeem our loss. Alleluia!

Hymns of praise then let us sing, Alleluia!
Unto Christ, our heavenly King, Alleluia!
Who endured the Cross and grave, Alleluia!
Sinners to redeem and save. Alleluia!

But the pains that he endured, Alleluia!
Our salvation have procured; Alleluia!
Now above the sky he's King, Alleluia!
Where the angels ever sing. Alleluia!

[Lyra Davidica, 1708]

MORNING PRAYER

God of the night and of the morning: the day of resurrection has dawned upon us, the day of true light and life, on which Christ, the life of believers, arose from the dead. We give You thanks and praise, O God. As we celebrate the day of our Lord's resurrection, bestow on us quiet peace and special gladness; so that being blessed from morning to night by your favoring mercy, we may rejoice in the gift of our Redeemer. **Amen.**

[Mozarabic Sacramentary, 7th c.]

PSALTER   Psalm 114

SCRIPTURE

Year A: Mt. 28: 1-10
Year B: Mk. 16: 1-8
Year C: Lk. 24: 1-12

CANTICLE OF ZECHARIAH (*Benedictus*, see page 20 or *UMH* 209)

PRAYERS OF INTERCESSION AND SUPPLICATION

God of power and majesty, with the rising of the sun you have raised Jesus Christ and delivered him and us all from death's destruction. We praise you on this bright day for all your gifts of new life. Especially we thank you:

for all victories over sin in our lives...
for loyalty and love of friends and family...
for the newborn, the newly baptized, and those
now in your eternal home...
for the renewal of nature...
for the continuing witness of the church in Christ...

God of eternity, you are present with us because of Christ's rising from the dead, and you persist in lifting

us to new life in him. We bring to you our prayers for this world in need of resurrection. Especially we pray:
for nations and peoples in strife...
for the poor and impoverished, at home and abroad...
for those we know in particular circumstances of distress...
for the diseased and dying...
for all who follow the risen Christ...

[FROM DAILY PRAYER, PCUSA]

COLLECT

O Christ our God, though you went down into the grave, yet you put down the power of hades and rose a conqueror: speak to us as you spoke to the myrrh-bearing women, bidding us rejoice; give us peace as you bestowed peace upon your apostles, and grant us the joy of resurrection. **Amen.**   [ORTHODOX, alt DWV]

THE LORD'S PRAYER

HYMN   [87.87 D; tune: *HYFRYDOL, UMH* 196]

Alleluia! Alleluia!
Hearts to heaven and voices raise;
Sing to God a hymn of gladness,
Sing to God a hymn of praise:
He who on the Cross a Victim
For the world's salvation bled,
Jesus Christ, the King of Glory,
Now is risen from the dead.

Christ is risen, Christ the first fruits
Of the holy harvest field,
Which with all its full abundance
At his second coming yield;
Then the golden ears of harvest
Will their heads before him wave,
Ripened by his glorious sunshine,
From the furrows of the grave.

Christ is risen, we are risen;
Shed upon us heavenly grace,
Rain, and dew, and gleams of glory
From the brightness of thy face;
That we, with our hearts in heaven,
Here on earth may fruitful be,
Then with all your saints be gathered,
And be ever, Lord with thee.

Alleluia! Alleluia!
Glory be to God on high;
Alleluia to the Savior,
Who has gained the victory;
Alleluia to the Spirit,
Fount of love and sanctity;
Alleluia! Alleluia!
To the Triune Majesty.

[BISHOP CHR. WORDSWORTH, 1807-1885; ALT]

DISMISSAL AND BLESSING

Now may the God of peace who brought back from the dead our Lord Jesus, the great shepherd of the sheep, by the blood of the eternal covenant, make you complete in everything good so that you may do his will, working among us that which is pleasing in his sight, through Jesus Christ, to whom be the glory forever and ever!

(HEBREWS 13:20-21)

Amen! Alleluia! Alleluia!

[ADAPTED FROM HEBREWS 13:20-21; TAR]

PASCHAL VESPERS

[This office, centering in the remembrance of the renewal of the baptismal covenant and the Emmaus experience, is a quiet service of great beauty with which to conclude the triduum. It replaces both Evening Prayer and Compline on the evening of Easter day. It is centered around three "stations:" the paschal candle (which should still be burning); the baptismal font; and the Lord's table.]

GATHERING AROUND THE PASCHAL CANDLE
    Jesus Christ is the light of the world,
        No darkness can overcome his light.
    Stay with us, Lord, for it is evening,
        and the day is almost over.
    Be our companion in the way, kindle our hearts, and awaken hope, that we may know you as you are revealed in Scripture and the breaking of bread. Grant this for the sake of your love. **Amen.**   [BCP; ALT ELE; DWV]

HYMN OF LIGHT   (*Phos hilaron,* see page 8)

THANKSGIVING FOR THE LIGHT
    Blessed are you, O Lord our God. In every age you have written our history in water. From the chaos of the seas you brought forth our world. From the midst of the Red Sea you gave birth to a people. Through the Jordan you brought Israel to a promised land and sent forth your Son to be the anointed who would proclaim the good news of your kingdom. In these days you have again recreated and formed us. In the memorial of Christ's death and rising, new sons and daughters have been born from the font, the womb of your church. Keep alive in all of us the joy of this season that always and everywhere the Easter alleluia may arise as a hymn of glory to your name. All power and glory be to you through Jesus our risen Lord in the life-giving love of the Holy Spirit this eventide and for ever and ever. **Amen.**

[FROM *TRIDUUM SOURCEBOOK*]

Let us pray for unity and peace in God's service.
Let us pray for pardon, peace and protection.

EVENING PRAYER CANTICLE (Ps. 141)   (see page 9)

COLLECT
God of life and light, you have renewed us with your
Holy Spirit through the celebration of the paschal mystery. May we live as those restored by water and the
Spirit through Christ's dying and rising again so that we
might be led with all your people to feast at the paschal
banquet in your presence forever. Through Jesus Christ
our Lord who lives and reigns with you and the Holy
Spirit, one God forever and ever. **Amen.**   [DWV]

FIRST LESSON Isaiah 55

PSALM 150

PROCESSION TO THE FONT

HYMN "Praise and Thanksgiving Be to God" (*UMH* 604)

*(The water in the font is touched in remembrance of the renewal
of baptismal vows in the Great Paschal Vigil)*

SECOND LESSON Romans 6:8-11

THE CANTICLE OF MARY (*Magnificat,* see p 8,*UMH* 197 st. 4 or 198-
200)

PRAYERS OF INTERCESSION AND SUPPLICATION
In peace, let us pray to the Lord.
For peace from on high and for the salvation of our souls...

That the Lord Jesus Christ, our Savior, may grant us
triumph and victory over the temptations of our visible
and invisible enemies...

That Christ may raise us with him and make us rise from the tomb of our sins and offenses...

That Christ may fill us with the joy and happiness of his holy resurrection...

That we may receive as a guest the one who becomes our host at table in the breaking of bread, and rejoice beyond limit, together with the hosts of saints glorified through him in the church triumphant in heaven...

Help us, save us, have mercy on us, and protect us, O God, by your grace. For you are our Light and our Resurrection, O Christ our God. We give glory to you and to your eternal Father and to your all-holy, good and life-giving Spirit, now and always and for ever and ever. Amen. [ADAPTED FROM THE ORTHODOX LITURGY]

THE LORD'S PRAYER

PROCESSION TO THE LORD'S TABLE

HYMN "O Thou Who This Mysterious Bread" (*UMH* 613)

THIRD LESSON Luke 24:13-35
--silence--

[Here bread (either remaining from an earlier celebration of the eucharist or a new loaf) may be lifted up, and then broken into as many pieces as there are participants in the service. Each person then shares with all others in:

THE SHARING OF BREAD AND THE KISS OF PEACE

NIGHT COLLECT
O God, the eternal light, the Splendor of the stars, the Clearness of the night, the Enlightener of the darkness: grant us to pass this night in security and peace; hear our prayers through Jesus Christ, the bread of heaven. **Amen.** [MOZARABIC, BEFORE 700 A.D.; ADAPTED DTB]

BLESSING AND DISMISSAL

Let us go forth in the name of Christ whose resurrection has brought us new life, and the grace of our Lord Jesus Christ and the love of God and the koinonia of the Holy Spirit will be us now and always.

Thanks be to God!
Alleluia! Alleluia!! Alleluia!!!   [TAR]

INDEX OF HYMN-TEXTS